dangerous
desserts

Over 200 tried-and-tested recipes

dangerous
desserts

Quadrille Publishing

Contents

First published in 1998 by
Quadrille Publishing Limited,
Alhambra House,
27–31 Charing Cross Road,
London WC2H 0LS

Reprinted in 1999, 2000 (twice)

The material in this volume was previously published in *BBC Good Food* and *BBC Vegetarian Good Food* magazines.

Text © The contributors 1998
Photography © The photographers 1998
(For a full list of contributors and photographers see page 172.)
Design & Layout © 1998 Quadrille Publishing Limited

ISBN 1 899988 23 8

Editor & Project Manager: Lewis Esson
Editorial Director: Jane O'Shea
Art Director: Mary Evans
Design: Paul Welti
Project Editor for the BBC: Jane Parsons
Production: Candida Jackson
Typesetting: Peter Howard

Set in Fenice and Futura
Printed and bound in Singapore by KHL Printing Co Pte Ltd
Colour separations by Colourscan, Singapore

Throughout the book both metric and imperial quantities are given. Use either all metric or all imperial, as the two are not necessarily interchangeable.

Introduction

Everyone with a taste for the wicked and wonderful needs this lavish new cookbook compiled from *BBC Good Food* and *BBC Vegetarian Good Food* magazines. Over 200 recipes guide you through the creation of a vast range of sweets and puddings – some so simple you can whip them up in seconds, others guaranteed to make your guests gasp in astonishment. There are dishes for all occasions, all budget levels and all seasons – including many that can be made well ahead of time, so there is no last-minute panic and the cook can enjoy the meal as much as everyone else.

Every recipe has been tried and tested by the *BBC Good Food* or *BBC Vegetarian Good Food* teams in the magazines' test kitchens and a wealth of sumptuous photographs shows the end-results in all their glory. Most chapters also feature at least one master class, illustrated with full-colour step-by-step photographs, showing exactly how to make such classics as crème brûlée, cheesecake, pavlova and roulade. Because everything is explained with such care and expertise, in the magazines' characteristic clear and user-friendly way, it makes no difference whether you are a beginner or a professional pastry chef – this book should be on every cook's shelf.

A slice from Phil Vickery's glorious whole bitter chocolate pudding with chocolate fudge sauce, see page 111.

Whipping up a Storm

A seductive selection of soufflés, mousses and meringues

Apple soufflé

Here the plain baked apple gets a makeover, to become a budding starlet.

Serves 6

9 large eating apples
1 tbsp fresh lemon juice
20g/¾oz butter
1 tsp ground cinnamon
50g/1¾oz caster sugar
3 eggs, separated
icing sugar, for dusting

for the caramelized apples

50g/1¾oz butter
50g/1¾oz caster sugar
1 tsp finely grated lemon rind
1 tbsp fresh lemon juice
2 tbsp brandy or Calvados (optional)
single cream

1 Preheat the oven to 190°C / 375°F / gas 5. Bring the eggs to room temperature before you whisk them to give more volume. Slice off the stalk end of six apples. Then cut around the top edge of each apple and scoop out the flesh, leaving about a 1cm / ½ inch border.
2 Brush all the cut edges of the apple cups with lemon juice to prevent discoloration. Roughly chop the flesh and place in a pan with one tablespoon of water. Cover and cook for 5–8 minutes until the apples are softened. Remove from the heat and press through a sieve into a bowl.
3 Beat the butter into the apple purée, then stir in the cinnamon, sugar and egg yolks. In a clean, dry, grease-free bowl whisk the egg whites until stiff and dry. Fold a quarter into the apple mix, then fold in the remainder using a metal spoon, cutting through the mixture until evenly mixed.
4 Place the apple cups in an ovenproof dish,

using scrunched foil to keep them stable, if necessary. Carefully spoon in the soufflé mixture and bake for 20–25 minutes until well risen and golden brown.
5 Make the caramelized apples: peel, core and quarter the remaining apples, then cut each quarter into four slices. Melt the butter in a shallow pan, add the apples and cook quickly, turning once, until light golden. Stir in the sugar, lemon rind and juice; simmer for a few minutes until syrupy. Keep warm until the soufflés are ready.
6 If using brandy or Calvados, add it to the caramelized apples, ignite carefully and serve when the flames have disappeared. Place one apple soufflé on each warm serving plate with a small pile of the hot caramelized apples and some cream. Dust the soufflés with icing sugar and serve immediately.

Hot lemon soufflés

Sharp and sweet, these inexpensive little fruit cups make the most sophisticated last course.

Serves 6

8 large lemons
15g/½oz butter, plus more for the
  dish
175g/6oz caster sugar
200ml/7fl oz milk
2 eggs, separated
1 tbsp plain flour
icing sugar, for dusting

1 Preheat the oven to 200°C / 400°F / gas 6 and butter an ovenproof dish. Slice the tops off 6 of the lemons and scoop out the flesh and membranes. Strain this pulp through a sieve and reserve the juice. Cut a thin slice off the base of each of the 6 lemons, then stand them close together in the buttered dish.
2 Put the lemon juice and half of the sugar in a pan. Bring to the boil, stirring until the sugar has dissolved, then boil for 2-3 minutes until slightly syrupy. Stir in the butter and keep this sauce warm.
3 Pare the rind from one of the remaining lemons and place the rind in a pan with the milk. Heat gently, then simmer for 2 minutes; remove the pared rind. Grate the zest from the last lemon and reserve.
4 Whisk the egg yolks and half the remaining sugar until pale and slightly thickened. Whisk in

the flour, then strain in the milk. Bring the milk mixture slowly to the boil in a pan, stirring until thickened and smooth. Remove from the heat and stir in grated lemon zest.
5 Whisk the egg whites until foamy, add the remaining sugar and whisk until stiff. Then fold into the custard mixture. Divide the mixture among the lemon shells and bake for 15-20 minutes, until well risen and golden. Dust with icing sugar.
6 Pour the sauce on 6 plates and quickly place a soufflé in the centre of each. Serve at once.

Chocolate praline soufflé with marinated summer fruits

The luxury of the best chocolate truffles in a melting soufflé, set off with summer berries for an evening to remember.

Serves 4

for the praline
50g/2oz flaked almonds
85g/3oz granulated sugar

for the soufflé(s)
20g/¾oz butter, cubed, plus more
    for the dish(es)
25g/1oz cornflour
150ml/¼pint milk
75g/2¾oz caster sugar
1tsp vanilla extract
4 eggs, separated
75g/2¾oz dark chocolate, chopped

to serve
250g/9oz summer fruits
2tbsp crème de cassis (optional)
icing sugar, for dusting

1 Preheat the oven to 200°C/400°F/gas 6. Make the praline: line a baking sheet with foil. Toast the almonds in a dry frying pan until golden brown. Put the sugar in a pan with 2 tablespoons of cold water and heat gently, stirring, until completely dissolved. Without stirring, boil rapidly until the syrup turns the colour of toffee. Immediately remove from the heat and stir in the toasted almonds, then turn out on a baking sheet. Allow to cool for about 15 minutes, then break into pieces. Reserve 8 nicely shaped pieces and whiz the rest in a food processor or blender until reduced to coarse crumbs.

2 Generously butter four 300ml/½pint soufflé dishes or one 1.25 litre/2pint dish. In a pan, blend the cornflour with 3 tablespoons of the milk. Add the remaining milk and the sugar, and cook over a moderate heat, stirring all the time, until the sauce thickens. Remove from the heat and stir in the butter, praline crumbs, vanilla and egg yolks.

3 In a clean dry, grease-free bowl, whisk the egg whites until they form stiff peaks. Fold one-quarter of the egg whites into the sauce, then fold in the chocolate, followed by the remaining egg whites.

4 Pour the mixture into the prepared dish(es) and set on a baking sheet. Bake in the oven for 25 minutes for the smaller soufflés or 30-35 minutes for the larger one, until risen and golden brown.

5 Meanwhile, mix the summer fruits with the cassis, if you are using it. Remove the soufflé(s) from the oven and set on a plate or individual plates. Spoon the fruits around the soufflé(s) and decorate with the reserved praline pieces. Dust quickly with icing sugar and serve immediately.

Right: **Made in coffee cups, ramekins and even scooped-out fruit, individual soufflés, like the Dark mocha soufflés, come in all guises.**

Dark mocha soufflés with ice cream and mocha sauce

With the punch of strong coffee and the kick of brandy, these round off a dinner party perfectly.

Serves 6

butter, for greasing
1tbsp ground almonds
150g/5½ fl oz plain chocolate
4 tbsp strong black coffee
4 eggs, separated
2tsp plain flour
100g/3½ oz caster sugar
good quality ice cream, to serve

for the mocha sauce
100g/3½ oz plain chocolate
150ml/¼pint double cream
2tbsp strong black coffee
2tbsp brandy

1 Preheat the oven to 190°C/375°F/gas 5, Generously butter six 200ml/7fl oz ramekin dishes or ovenproof teacups. Lightly dust the insides with ground almonds. Bring the eggs to room temperature before you whisk them to give more volume.

2 Break up the chocolate in a bowl and add the coffee. Set over a pan of simmering water and stir gently until melted. Remove from the heat and leave to cool for a few minutes, then stir in the egg yolks, flour and half the sugar.

3 Whisk the egg whites in a clean, grease-free bowl. Whisk in the remaining sugar, one table-spoon at a time. Gently fold a quarter of the egg white mixture into the chocolate sauce; then fold in the remainder, cutting through the mixture with a metal spoon until evenly blended.

4 Divide the mixture between the prepared dishes and bake for 20–25 minutes until well risen.

5 Make the sauce: break up the chocolate in a pan, add the cream and coffee and blend over a low heat until smooth and shiny. Stir in the brandy and pour into a jug.

6 Serve the soufflés immediately. Each diner splits their soufflé, adds a scoop of ice cream and pours over some chocolate sauce.

Master class: making a soufflé

Candied fruit soufflés

Michel Roux shows how easy it is to get perfect soufflés every time.

Serves 4-6

25g/1oz softened butter
85g/3oz caster sugar, plus more for the
   dishes
115g/4oz mixed candied fruits (cherries,
   angelica, orange or lemon, apricots)
4tbsp milk
1 vanilla pod, split, or 1 coffee spoon of
   good-quality vanilla essence
20g/¾oz runny honey
whites of 7 eggs
8 vanilla-flavoured macaroons (optional)
2tbsp icing sugar
**for the crème pâtissière
(pastry cream)**
3 egg yolks
50g/2oz caster sugar
20g/¾oz flour (plain)
250ml/9fl oz milk
1 vanilla pod, split, or 1 coffee spoon of
   good-quality vanilla essence
a little butter or icing sugar, for cooling

1 First make the crème pâtissière: whisk the egg yolks with about one-third of the sugar until pale and of a light ribbon consistency. Sift in the flour and mix thoroughly. In a pan, bring the milk to the boil with the remaining sugar and the vanilla pod or essence. As soon as it begins to bubble, pour about one-third on the egg mixture, stirring continuously. Pour this back into the pan and bring to the boil over a very gentle heat, stirring continuously. Bubble for 2 minutes, then transfer to a bowl. Remove the vanilla pod, if using. Dot the surface with a few flakes of butter or dust it lightly with icing sugar to prevent a skin forming. These amounts makes about 375g/13oz; the pastry cream not used in the soufflé can be stored in the fridge for up to 36 hours. Use it for pastries or cakes, or a fruit dessert.

2 Brush the insides of 4-6 individual soufflé dishes, 10cm/4in diameter and 6cm/2⅜in deep, with the softened butter. Put 25g/1oz sugar into one dish and rotate to coat the inside. Tip excess sugar into the next dish (1) and repeat the operation to coat all the dishes. Preheat the oven to 220°C/425°F/gas 7 and place a baking sheet in the oven to heat.
3 Chop the candied fruits finely. Put the milk in a bowl and mix in the fruits. Scrape out the inside of the vanilla pod with the tip of a knife and stir it, or the essence, into the mixture. Place 175g/6oz of the pastry cream in a wide bowl and, if necessary, warm it to tepid in a microwave oven or bain-marie. Add the fruit mixture and honey.

4 Beat the egg whites until half-risen (2), then add the remaining sugar and beat until stiff. Use a whisk to fold one-third of the egg whites into the pastry cream (3), then add the rest and fold in with a spatula. Fill the soufflé dishes up to one-third full with the mixture, sprinkle two lightly crushed macaroons over each one, then fill up the dishes and smooth the surface with a palette knife. Ease the mixture away from the edge of the dishes with the tip of a knife (4).
5 Cook the soufflés: place the soufflé dishes on the preheated baking sheet and bake for 6-7 minutes.
6 To serve: dust each soufflé with a veil of icing sugar and place on individual plates.

Left: Dark chocolate mousse in a spiced tuile basket, served on a bed of raspberry sauce.

Above: Chilled Valentine's mousse made with white chocolate and lovingly decorated with cocoa-powder hearts.

Chilled Valentine's mousse

For one large mousse, Gary Rhodes cooks the sponge in a flan ring, wraps it in a paper collar and spoons the filling on top.

Serves 4

for the sponge

115g/4oz caster sugar
2 eggs, separated
25g/1oz cocoa powder
25g/1oz plain flour
2tbsp Kirsch liqueur (optional)

for the filling

400g/14oz griottine or canned
    cherries, drained, or 450g/1lb
    fresh cherries, stoned

for the mousse

400g/14oz dark or white chocolate,
    broken into pieces
25g/1oz liquid glucose or golden
    syrup
600ml/1 pint double cream
icing sugar or cocoa powder, for
    dusting

1 Make the sponge: preheat the oven to 160°C / 325°F / gas 3. Butter and line a 28x18cm / 11x7in Swiss roll pan. Whisk half of the sugar with the egg yolks until thick and pale. In a clean bowl, whisk the egg whites to soft peaks and then add the remaining sugar and whisk to a stiff meringue.
2 Sift the cocoa powder and flour into the egg yolk mixture and fold in. Whisk in a quarter of the meringue, then gently fold in the remaining meringue. Spread on the prepared pan to a thickness of 5mm-1cm / 1/4-1/2in. Bake for 20-25 minutes, then leave to cool.
3 Using a plain cutter, cut out four 7.5cm / 3in rounds of sponge and sit them in 9cm / 3 1/2in ramekins. (Use leftover sponge in a trifle.) Sprinkle a little Kirsch on the sponge if you like. If using griottine or canned cherries, drain them and place a few on top of each sponge. For fresh cherries, cook them in a little Kirsch or water with caster sugar until tender. (If you don't want

to use the liqueur, reserve the syrup from the cherries instead and sprinkle it over the sponge.)
4 Make the mousse: melt the chocolate in a bowl set over warm water. Remove from the heat and let cool for 5 minutes. Add the glucose or syrup.
5 Whip the cream until it has just thickened and holds its shape. Fold one-third into the melted chocolate, then fold in the remaining cream. Tie strips of greaseproof paper around the ramekins to come 4cm / 1 1/2in above the top and secure with tape. Spoon in the mousse so that it comes roughly 2.5cm / 1in above the ramekins. Smooth the tops and place in the fridge to set for 1-2 hours for dark chocolate and 3-4 if you are using white. Carefully remove the greaseproof paper.
6 Cut a heart shape from a thin piece of card. Hold the card over the dessert and dust lightly with icing sugar to make a heart. For a white chocolate dessert, make the heart by dusting with cocoa powder.

Dark chocolate mousse in a spiced tuile basket

The most elegant of presentations heralds a sophisticated flavour surprise. Serve it with the raspberry sauce on page 94.

Serves 4

55g/1 3/4oz white chocolate
raspberries and mint sprigs to garnish

for the chocolate mousse

175g/6oz dark chocolate
1 egg yolk
1tbsp brandy
15g/1/2 oz butter, melted
125ml/4fl oz double cream
whites of 2 medium eggs
1tbsp caster sugar

for the spiced tuiles

25g/1oz butter, plus extra for greasing
25g/1oz icing sugar
white of 1 small egg
25g/1oz plain flour
1/4 tsp each cinnamon, allspice and cloves

1 Melt the white chocolate in a heatproof bowl set over a pan of gently simmering water. Place the chocolate in a greaseproof paper icing bag. Pipe lacy 'cobwebs' of chocolate on a baking tray lined with non-stick baking paper. Chill until set.
2 To make the mousse, melt the dark chocolate in a heatproof bowl as above. Beat in the egg yolk, brandy, butter and 3 tablespoons of the cream.
3 In a large bowl, whip the remainder of the cream until it holds its own shape on the surface, then fold carefully into the chocolate mousse mix.
4 In a separate bowl, whisk the egg whites until they form soft peaks. Gradually whisk in the caster sugar and continue whisking until stiff but not dry. Gently fold the egg whites, a little at a time, into the chocolate mixture until well combined. Spoon the mousse into a large piping bag fitted with a star nozzle and set aside.

5 To make the tuiles, preheat the oven to 190°C / 375°F / gas 5, line a baking sheet with greaseproof paper and brush lightly with melted butter. In a bowl, cream the butter and icing sugar together. Add the egg white and whisk until smooth. Sift in the flour and spices and mix to a smooth batter.
6 Spread the batter into four 10cm / 4inch circles about the thickness of a 10p coin on the baking sheet, well apart to allow for spreading. Cook for 6-8 minutes until lightly browned. Allow to cool for a minute or so. Carefully peel one from the sheet with a palette knife and shape it over an upturned cup. Repeat to make three more. Work quickly to shape them while they're still warm.
7 To serve, place a tuile basket on each plate. Pipe tall swirls of mousse into each basket and top with white chocolate 'cobwebs'. Decorate with raspberries, mint sprigs and the raspberry sauce.

Apricot, rosemary and honey mousse

In Josceline Dimbleby's mousse, the wonderfully intense flavour of apricots is heightened by the delicate and unusual addition of fresh rosemary.

Serves 6

350g/12oz fresh apricots
3tbsp clear honey
juice of 2 lemons
2tsp finely chopped fresh rosemary
15g/½oz (1 sachet) powdered gelatine
4 large eggs, separated
pinch of salt
apricot slices and rosemary sprigs, to decorate

1 Halve the apricots, remove the stones and chop the flesh into small pieces. Place in a pan with the honey, lemon juice and rosemary. Bring to the boil, stirring continuously, until the honey melts, then simmer for 15-20 minutes, stirring once or twice, until the apricots are reduced to pulp. Set aside.
2 Sprinkle the gelatine over the hot apricot mixture and stir continuously for 2 minutes until it has completely dissolved.
3 Bring a medium pan of water to the boil, place the egg yolks in a heatproof bowl and set over the pan. Stir the apricot mixture into the egg yolks and cook gently for about 5 minutes, stirring continuously, until the mixture thickens. Remove from the heat and leave to cool.

4 Place the egg whites in a large bowl with the salt and whisk until they form soft peaks. Using a metal spoon, fold the egg whites into the apricot mixture. Spoon into a large glass dish and chill for at least 2 hours before serving.
5 Decorate with apricot slices and rosemary sprigs to serve.

Right: **Smooth sensuous Nectarine mousse, decorated with some halved strawberries and nectarine wedges, all glazed with apricot jam.**

Nectarine mousse

Deceptively light, this is the ultimate in cream cakes, with a full fruit flavour.

Serves 6-8

for the cake
2 eggs
50g/2oz caster sugar
50g/2oz plain flour
1tbsp cocoa powder
for the mousse
6 ripe nectarines
1tbsp powdered gelatine
3tbsp freshly squeezed orange juice
60-75g/2-3oz caster sugar
white of 1 egg
150ml/¼pint double cream
to finish
seasonal fruit, to decorate
2tbsp apricot jam, to glaze

1 Make the cake: preheat the oven to 200°C/400°F/gas 6. Grease and line a baking sheet with greaseproof paper, then mark two 20cm/8in circles on the paper. Whisk together the eggs and sugar for about 10 minutes until the mixture is thick and pale, and leaves a trail when the whisk is lifted. Sift the flour and fold in gently. Transfer half of the mixture to a separate bowl and sift in the cocoa powder; fold in lightly. Place alternate spoonfuls of the mixtures on the marked circles, spreading to the edges, then swirl together with a skewer. Bake for 10-12 minutes until the mixture is firm. Remove the paper and allow to cool on a wire rack.
2 Line an 18cm/7in round cake tin with plastic film. Using a sharp knife, trim the circles of sponge to fit the tin.

3 Make the mousse: skin, stone and purée the nectarines. Dissolve the gelatine in the orange juice in a small bowl set over a pan of hot water. Mix into the nectarine purée with the sugar. Whisk the egg white and whip the cream, then fold the egg white and cream into the purée.
4 Line the base of the cake pan with one of the sponge circles. Pour in the mousse, cover with the other sponge circle, then chill for several hours until set.
5 Turn out and decorate with fresh fruit. Warm the jam, push through a sieve, then brush over the fruit. Serve with loganberry sauce, if you like.

White and dark chocolate mousse

This easy-to-make black-and-white marbled mousse makes the most elegant of party desserts.

Serves 6-8

butter for the pan
175g/6oz Madeira cake
2tbsp brandy
1tbsp cold strong black coffee
175g/6oz plain chocolate, broken
   into pieces
175g/6oz white chocolate, broken
   into pieces
450ml/¾pint double cream

1 Grease a 20cm/8inch loose-bottomed cake pan and line the base with baking paper. Line the sides with strips of foil. Slice the Madeira cake and use it to line the bottom of the cake tin, cutting the pieces to fit. Mix the brandy with the coffee and drizzle this over the base.
2 Melt the two types of chocolate in separate heatproof bowls over pans of hot water. Whip the cream until it holds its shape, then divide it between two bowls. Stir the plain chocolate into one bowl and the white chocolate into the other.

3 Spoon alternating blobs of white and plain chocolate mixture into the cake pan and swirl them into one another with a skewer. Smooth over the top and then chill for at least 2 hours.
4 Carefully remove the mousse from the cake pan and peel off the foil. Place the mousse on a serving plate and chill again until ready to serve.

Variation:

Instead of the coffee and brandy, you can flavour this mousse with orange-flavoured liqueur,

Strawberry mousse

Try this mousse as the finale to an alfresco summer lunch – or even for a picnic.

Serves 8

350g/12oz strawberries, hulled
5tsp powdered gelatine
2 eggs, separated
2 tbsp cornflour
150ml/¼pint double cream
150ml/¼pint milk
100g/3½oz caster sugar
more strawberries, to decorate

1 Blend the strawberries to a purée in a food processor.
2 In a small bowl, sprinkle the gelatine over 3 tablespoons of cold water. (Never pour water over gelatine as it sets solid!) Leave to soak.
3 Place the egg yolks in a pan with the cornflour and stir with a wooden spoon until smooth. Gradually blend in the cream, milk and sugar. Bring to the boil, whisking constantly, until the mixture becomes thick and smooth. Stir in the softened gelatine and then beat in the strawberry purée.
4 In a clean dry grease-free bowl, beat the egg whites until they form soft peaks. Using a tablespoon, fold one-quarter of the egg whites into the strawberry mixture, then carefully fold in the rest.

5 Spoon into 8 individual moulds or one large mould and chill for several hours.
6 To unmould: loosen the edges of the mousse(s) carefully with a knife then dip briefly in very hot water and invert on a serving plate. Decorate with strawberries.

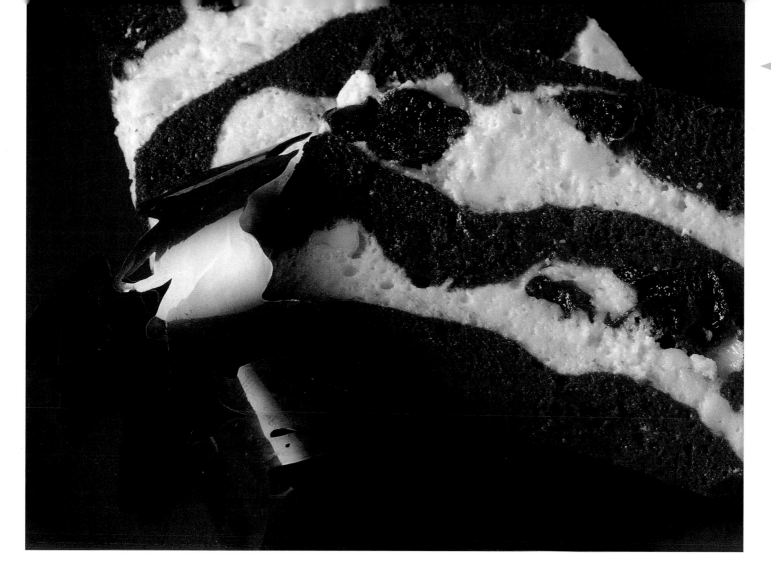

Chocolate marquise slice

This substantial layered chocolate terrine makes an impressive buffet table centrepiece.

Serves 8

150g/5oz no-soak pitted prunes,
   roughly sliced
3tbsp brandy
1tbsp powdered gelatine
200g/7oz plain chocolate, broken
   into pieces
150g/5oz white chocolate, broken
   into pieces
4 tbsp milk
225ml/8fl oz double cream
2tbsp cocoa powder
whites of 6 eggs
100g/4oz caster sugar

for the ribbons

100g/3½oz plain chocolate

1 Line a 900g/2lb loaf pan with plastic film so that it fits into the corners and hangs over the edges. Place the prunes in the brandy to soak. Sprinkle half the gelatine over 2 tablespoons of cold water in a bowl; repeat the process in another bowl with the remaining gelatine.

2 Melt the two chocolates in separate bowls each with half the milk, either in the microwave or set over hot water. Stir half the cream into each bowl until smooth, then add the cocoa to the plain chocolate.

3 Place each bowl of gelatine over a pan containing a little simmering water until the gelatine dissolves. Whisk one mixture into the plain chocolate, the other into the white.

4 Put the egg whites and sugar in a large bowl and sit this over a pan of simmering water. Beat with an electric whisk for 5 minutes until it forms a stiff, glossy meringue.

5 Spoon half the meringue into another bowl and gently fold the plain chocolate into it. Repeat with the white chocolate and prunes with their soaking liquid. Leave until they are beginning to set.

6 Spoon half the plain chocolate into the base of the prepared loaf pan, then half the white, then repeat the layers.

7 Freeze for several hours until firm.

8 Make the chocolate ribbons: melt the chocolate. Cut ten 15x5cm/6x2in rectangles of Perspex. Spread a little melted chocolate on one rectangle, swirling it decoratively near the edges with the tip of a spoon. Bring two short ends together, with the chocolate inside, to form a ring; secure with sticky tape. Repeat and leave to set. Hold the ends of the Perspex together so the chocolate doesn't crack, cut the tape and remove gently.

9 Turn out the marquise, cut it into thick slices and decorate with the chocolate ribbons.

Master class: making pavlova

Fruit pavlova

The pavlova was created in honour of the Russian prima ballerina Anna Pavlova when she visited Australia and New Zealand in the 1920s. The perfect pavlova is crisp on the outside and yet soft — almost marshmallow-like — on the inside.

Serves 6

butter for greasing
whites of 4 eggs
225g/8oz caster sugar
1 tsp white wine vinegar
1 tsp cornflour
for the filling
175ml/6fl oz double cream
1 tbsp icing sugar
1 tbsp Marsala or dry sherry (optional)
250g/9oz mascarpone cheese
100g/3½oz strawberries
100g/3½oz raspberries
1 ripe peach, sliced

1 Preheat the oven to 130°C/275°F/gas 1. Lightly grease a baking tray and line it with non-stick baking paper. Using a plate as a guide, draw a 23cm/9in circle on it.
2 In a large, clean and dry bowl, whisk the egg whites until they form stiff peaks.
3 Gradually whisk in the caster sugar, a tablespoon at a time, until the mixture becomes thick and glossy. Then carefully fold in the white wine vinegar and the cornflour.
4 Spoon half the mixture on the baking paper to fill the circle, then drop large spoonfuls of the remaining mixture on top, adding more to the edges to form a high rim.
5 Place meringue in centre of oven. After 5 minutes, lower to 120°C/250°F/gas ½. Bake for 50 minutes, then turn oven off without opening the door. Leave meringue in the oven for at least 3 hours or overnight to cool completely. Transfer to a wire rack and remove baking paper. Place on a large serving plate.
6 To make the filling: whip the cream with the sugar, then fold in the Marsala or sherry, if

using it, and the mascarpone. Spoon into the meringue case and pile the fruit on top. Keep cool, but do not refrigerate, before serving.

Top tips for meringue
* Set the temperature of the oven very low so the meringue cooks slowly and remains white.
* Use eggs at room temperature, not straight from the fridge, and be careful not to leave any trace of yolk in the whites.
* Whisk the egg whites in a spotlessly clean bowl; the slightest trace of grease will prevent them from whisking to full volume.
* The egg whites must be whisked well between additions of sugar. If you rush this stage, a syrupy liquid may separate out.

* The addition of white wine vinegar (or lemon juice) and cornflour will ensure that the meringue turns out soft and fluffy inside.

Flavouring meringue
To give meringue a special flavour, carefully fold in the following when preparing the meringue mixture, before shaping and baking:
* coarsely grated chocolate — it melts lusciously into the meringue as it bakes.
* ground or coarsely chopped hazelnuts, almond or other nuts — toast them before use to give a wonderful taste and texture to the meringue.
* finely grated orange and/or lemon zest give the meringue a zing.

Meringue peaches

Give canned fruit the luxury treatment for a dessert to remember.

Serves 4

400g/14oz canned peach halves,
 drained
8 amaretti biscuits, macaroons or any
 other small crunchy biscuits
2-3tbsp Cointreau or Grand Marnier
white of 1 egg
50g/2oz caster sugar
25g/1oz flaked almonds
icing sugar, for dusting
4 physalis fruits (cape gooseberries),
 to decorate

1 Preheat the oven to 200°C/400°F/gas 6. Pat the peaches dry on kitchen paper and place, hollow side up, on a baking sheet. Place one amaretti biscuit inside each hollow and drizzle over the Cointreau or Grand Marnier.
2 Whisk the egg white in a bowl until stiff, then gradually whisk in the sugar until it has a glossy appearance.
3 Use to fill a piping bag fitted with a star-shaped nozzle and pipe the meringue in a swirl over each peach.
4 Sprinkle over the almonds and bake for about 10 minutes or until the meringue is a pale golden brown.
5 Lightly dust the meringues with the icing sugar and serve on individual plates decorated with the physalis.

Passion fruit islands

Custard flavoured with exotic passion fruit is moulded into heart shapes and dressed with caramel.

Serves 2

for the custard
5 passion fruit
3 egg yolks
70g/2½oz caster sugar
2tsp cornflour
450ml/¾pint milk
2tbsp Cointreau or orange-flavoured
 liqueur (optional)
for the caramel
50g/2oz caster sugar
for the meringue
white of 1 egg
25g/1oz caster sugar
300ml/½pint milk

1 Make the custard: cut 4 passion fruit in half and press the pulp through a sieve to extract the juice. Reserve the juice. Beat together the egg yolks, sugar and cornflour until pale and creamy.
2 In a pan, bring the milk to the boil, then pour it into the egg mixture. Return the mixture to the pan and cook over a low heat, stirring, for about 15 minutes until thickened; do not allow to boil. Remove from the heat and cover the surface with greaseproof paper to prevent a skin forming. Leave to cool.
3 When cool, stir in the passion fruit juice and the liqueur, if using, then pour the custard into two shallow serving dishes.
4 Make the caramel: wrap a piece of greaseproof paper around a rolling pin. Heat the sugar in a small heavy-based pan with 3 tablespoons of water until dissolved. Bring to the boil, then boil rapidly until the syrup has turned deep golden. Immerse the base of the pan in cold water to prevent further cooking. Using a teaspoon, drizzle the caramel in streaks over the rolling pin. (If the caramel runs off the pin, leave it to cool for 30 seconds). Leave to set.
5 Make the meringue: whisk the egg white until stiff. Gradually whisk in the sugar, a little at a time, until the mixture is stiff and glossy.
6 In a small frying pan, heat the milk to a gentle simmer. Place a large heart-shaped cutter on a sheet of greaseproof paper and fill with about one-quarter of the meringue. Peel away the paper and cook the meringue in the milk for 1 minute. Flip the cutter over and cook for a further minute. Drain the meringue and lift away the cutter. Make three more hearts in the same way.
7 Cut the remaining passion fruit into quarters. Place the custards on serving plates and place two meringues on top of each. Arrange caramel pieces on top and decorate with the passion fruit quarters.

Cherry and almond queen of puddings

This storecupboard dessert will impress unexpected guests and makes a good last-minute family treat.

Serves 6

25g/1oz butter
55g/1¾oz fresh breadcrumbs
55g/1¾oz ground almonds
finely grated zest of 1 lemon
200g/7oz caster sugar
300ml/½pint single cream
300ml/½pint milk
1tsp almond essence
3 eggs, separated
675g/1½lb jar of stoned red cherries
4tsp cornflour
ground almonds, for sprinkling

1 Preheat the oven to 180°C/350°F/gas 4. Lightly butter a 1.4litre/2½ pint pie dish. Mix the breadcrumbs, almonds, lemon zest and 25g/1oz of the caster sugar in a bowl.
2 In a pan, heat the remaining butter, cream, milk and almond essence until the butter has melted. Pour over breadcrumb mixture. Set aside for 10 minutes, then beat in the egg yolks. Pour into the pie dish. Bake for 20 minutes until lightly set.
3 In a pan, blend 4 tablespoons of juice from the cherries with the cornflour. Add a further 150ml/¼ pint of the juice and cook, stirring, for 3-4 minutes. Drain the cherries and add to the pan. Spoon over the custard.
4 Increase the oven temperature to 200°C/400°F/gas 6. Whisk the egg whites until stiff. Gradually add the remaining caster sugar, whisking well

after each addition. Spoon the meringue over the cherries and sprinkle with ground almonds. Bake for 8-10 minutes, until lightly browned.

Left: Halving the strawberries before putting them in place makes it easier to serve such a dramatically appealing portion of Mississippi meringue pie.

Mississippi meringue pie

Fresh strawberries and a meringue topping turn this simple refrigerator cake into a Southern belle.

Serves 12

125g/4½oz butter
3tbsp chocolate hazelnut spread
350g/12oz chocolate digestive biscuits, crushed

for the filling
1tbsp powdered gelatine
6tbsp warm water
250g/9oz caster sugar
2tbsp cornflour
3 medium eggs, separated
450ml/¾pint single cream
1tbsp instant coffee granules
200g/7oz plain chocolate
150ml/¼pint double cream, whipped
675g/1½lb strawberries, hulled

1 In a large pan, gently melt the butter and chocolate spread. Stir in the crushed biscuits and mix well. Press the mixture into the base and sides of a deep 20cm/8in fluted loose-bottomed flan tin. Chill until ready to use.
2 Sprinkle the gelatine over the warm water in a small bowl and leave to soak for 5 minutes. In another small bowl, mix one-third of the caster sugar with the cornflour, egg yolks and a little of the single cream to form a smooth paste. In a pan, gently heat the remaining single cream with the coffee and chocolate, broken into pieces, until the chocolate has melted. Stir in the cornflour mixture and cook gently, stirring, until the custard has thickened enough to coat the back of a wooden spoon.
3 Set the gelatine mixture over a pan of simmering water and heat until dissolved. Stir into the

hot custard and allow to cool slightly. Fold in the whipped cream and pour the mixture into the biscuit case. Chill until set.
4 Preheat the grill to hot. Whisk the egg whites until stiff and gradually whisk in the remaining caster sugar until thick and glossy. Arrange the prepared strawberries over the chocolate filling. Spoon the meringue over to cover fully and grill for 3-4 minutes until browned.

Hazelnut, banana and caramel nests

This dessert is an object lesson in how to put on a show with the simplest of ingredients.

Serves 4

for the meringue
whites of 2 eggs
100g/3½oz caster sugar
¼ tsp white wine vinegar
¼ tsp cornflour
25g/1oz toasted hazelnuts, finely chopped
for the filling
3 ripe bananas, roughly chopped
1tbsp lemon juice
125ml/4fl oz Greek-style yoghurt
2tbsp maple syrup
for the caramel topping
50g/2oz caster sugar

1 Preheat the oven to 120°C/250°F/gas ½. Line a baking sheet with non-stick baking paper.
2 In a large clean and dry, grease-free bowl, whisk the egg whites until they form stiff peaks. Gradually whisk in the caster sugar, a tablespoon at a time, until the mixture becomes thick and glossy. Then carefully fold in the white wine vinegar and the cornflour, followed by the toasted hazelnuts.
3 Place a 1cm/½in plain nozzle in a large piping bag. Spoon the mixture into the bag and pipe four 10cm/4in rounds on the paper. Pipe another line of mixture around the edge of the rounds to create nests.
4 Place the meringue nests in the oven and bake for 1 hour until they are crisp. Remove from the paper and leave to cool on a wire rack.
5 Make the filling: toss the bananas with the lemon juice, then stir them into the yoghurt with the maple syrup. Spoon into the middle of each nest.
6 Make the caramel topping: place the sugar in a small saucepan and heat gently until it starts to melt. Swirl the pan around so the sugar melts evenly, then continue cooking until the contents of the pan have a light caramel colour. Remove from the heat and leave to stand for a few minutes.
7 Line a baking sheet with non-stick baking paper and, using a tablespoon, trail thin threads of the caramel over the paper in a criss-cross pattern; continue until all the syrup is used. Leave to cool until crisp. Peel the paper away from the caramel and use it to decorate the top of each basket. Serve immediately.

Saffron meringues with lemon syllabub

Spice up your meringues with the magical flavour and colour of saffron.

Serves 6

pinch of saffron strands
whites of 2 eggs
100g/3½oz caster sugar
¼ tsp white wine vinegar
¼ tsp cornflour

for the lemon syllabub

grated zest and juice of ½ lemon
2 tbsp dry sherry
25g/1oz caster sugar
150ml/¼pint double cream

1 Preheat the oven to 120°C/250°F/gas ½ and line a baking sheet with non-stick baking paper. Place the saffron strands in a small bowl, pour 1 tablespoon of boiling water over them and leave to infuse.

2 In a large clean and dry, grease-free bowl, whisk the egg whites until they form stiff peaks. Gradually whisk in the caster sugar, a tablespoon at a time, until the mixture becomes thick and glossy. Then carefully fold in the white wine vinegar and the cornflour.

3 Drain the saffron and carefully fold the soaked strands into the meringue mixture to create a streaked effect, being careful not to over-whip.

4 Using 2 tablespoons, shape the mixture into 12 oval mounds on the prepared baking sheet. Bake for 1 hour, until crisp on the outside and chewy inside. Turn off the oven and leave to cool in the oven for 1 hour.

5 Make the lemon syllabub: place the lemon juice and zest and the sherry in a large bowl and stir in the sugar until dissolved. Stir in the cream and beat for about 4-5 minutes, until forming soft peaks. Chill until required.

6 Sandwich pairs of meringue ovals with the syllabub filling and serve immediately.

The caramel topping for the hazelnut, banana and caramel nest opposite can be used to give a touch of grandeur to the simplest of desserts, even a dish of plain fruit.

Exotic fruit layer (See the picture on page 8)

The creamy exotic fruit filling and cardamom-flavoured meringue make this a fitting finale to a spicy meal.

Serves 6

whites of 3 eggs
175g/6oz caster sugar
1tsp lemon juice
1tsp cornflour
1tbsp crushed cardamom seeds,
   pods removed

for the filling

300ml/½pint double cream, lightly
   whipped
1 papaya, roughly chopped
1 mango, roughly chopped
2 passion fruit
coconut flakes, toasted, to decorate

1 Preheat the oven to 150°C/300°F/gas 2. Line 2 baking sheets with non-stick baking paper and draw on them three 11x23cm/4½x9in rectangles (2 on one, 1 on the other).

2 In a large clean and dry, grease-free bowl, whisk the egg whites until they form stiff peaks. Gradually whisk in the caster sugar, a tablespoon at a time, until the mixture becomes thick and glossy. Then carefully fold in the lemon juice and the cornflour, followed by the crushed cardamom seeds.

3 Spoon the meringue mixture on the rectangles on the prepared baking sheets and spread evenly. Place in the oven, reduce the setting to 130°C/275°F/gas 1 and bake for an hour. Turn off the oven and leave the meringues in the oven until cold.

4 Remove the meringues from the baking sheets and peel off the paper. Arrange one rectangle on a serving plate and spoon half the cream on top. Sandwich a second meringue rectangle on top, followed by a layer of half the fruits and the remaining cream. Place the final meringue rectangle on top and top with remaining fruits. Scatter over the coconut flakes. Cut into slices and serve immediately.

Variation:

Instead of cardamom, flavour the meringue with saffron as above or 2 teaspoons of finely chopped candied ginger.

Meringue Christmas tree

Season's beatings for an original edible table decoration.

Serves 6-8

whites of 4 eggs
225g/8oz icing sugar, sifted
300ml/1/2 pint double cream
275g/10oz thick Greek yoghurt

for decoration

1 star fruit
2 clementines
100g/3 1/2 oz caster sugar
100g/3 1/2 oz small seedless green or
    red grapes
a few cranberries (optional)

1 Preheat the oven to 120ºC/250ºF/gas 1/2. Line 3 baking sheets with baking paper. Mark on the paper circles with the following diameters: 5cm/2in; 7.5cm/3in; 10cm/4in; 12.5cm/5in; 15cm/6in; 17.5cm/7in.

2 Place the egg whites and icing sugar in a large clean dry, grease-free bowl set over a pan of simmering water. Using an electric whisk, beat the eggs and sugar for 10 minutes until the mixture is stiff and stands in soft peaks.

3 Remove the bowl from the heat and continue whisking for 2-3 minutes. Spoon the meringue mixture over the marked circles on the baking sheets, shaping the edges into curves. Peak the centre of the smallest meringue and the edges of the remaining ones.

4 Bake the meringues for 1 1/2 hours until very pale golden, then turn off the oven and leave them in the oven to finish cooking in the residual heat.

5 Prepare the decoration: slice the star fruit and segment the clementines. Gently heat half of the sugar in a small pan with two tablespoons of water until the sugar has dissolved. Increase the heat, then boil rapidly for 2-3 minutes until the syrup has turned a golden caramel.

6 Remove the caramel from the heat and leave until the bubbles subside. Spear the clementines, grapes and cranberries, if using them, on a fork and dip them into the caramel to coat. Transfer to a sheet of foil to set. Continue until all of the fruit is coated — do not coat the star fruit.

7 Whip the cream until stiff, then fold in the yoghurt. Reserve one small slice of star fruit. Set the largest meringue on a plate and spread with a little cream. Arrange some of the fruit over the cream and cover with the next largest meringue round. Continue layering the meringue, cream and fruit, finishing with the smallest meringue.

8 Just before serving, place the remaining sugar in a small clean pan with 2 tablespoons of water and make a caramel as before. Let cool for 5 minutes, then stick the reserved star fruit to the top of the cake with a little of the caramel. Using a metal spoon, lift a little more caramel out of the pan, dip the back of a fork into this and pull up quickly to form strands. Wrap these quickly around the tree. Repeat until all the caramel is used and the tree is evenly covered in strands.

9 Serve within 1 hour. The undecorated meringues will keep in a tin for up to a week.

Redcurrant meringue roulade

The sweet-sourness of the redcurrants and the yoghurt gives this roulade a very sophisticated edge.

Serves 8

whites of 3 eggs
1 tsp vanilla essence
1 tsp cornflour
1 tsp white wine vinegar
225g/8oz caster sugar
25g/1oz toasted hazelnuts, finely
    chopped
175g/6oz redcurrants
150ml/1/4 pint double cream
150g/5oz thick Greek yoghurt

1 Preheat the oven to 130ºC/275ºF/gas 1. Line a shallow 23x32.5cm/9x13in oblong cake tin with greaseproof paper.

2 Whisk the egg whites in a clean dry, grease-free bowl until stiff. Blend together the vanilla essence, cornflour and vinegar. Whisk 175g/6oz of the sugar into the egg whites, a tablespoon at a time, adding a little of the vanilla mixture with each addition. Whisk the mixture until it is stiff and marshmallowy.

3 Spread the mixture over the prepared cake tin and sprinkle with the nuts. Bake for 40 minutes, then remove from the oven and cover with foil.

4 Place the redcurrants with the remaining sugar and a tablespoon of water in a pan and cook for about 5 minutes until softened. Press through a nylon sieve and leave to cool. Whisk the cream until stiff, then fold in the yoghurt.

5 Turn the meringue out on a sheet of greaseproof paper. Spread with the cream mixture, then the redcurrant purée. Using the paper to help you, roll up the meringue from one short end. Transfer to a serving plate and chill for up to 2 hours before serving.

Hazelnut meringue roulade with mango and orange cream

The citrus zing of oranges brings out the best of the mango flavour for a memorable party dessert.

Serves 6-8

75g/3oz shelled hazelnuts
1tsp cornflour
1tsp vanilla extract
1tsp white wine vinegar
whites of 4 large eggs
150g/5oz caster sugar

for the filling
1 large or 2 medium ripe mangoes
2tbsp caster sugar
1tsp finely grated orange zest
200ml/7fl oz tub of crème fraîche

for the sauce
1 large ripe mango
2tbsp caster sugar
4-6tbsp orange juice

1 Preheat the oven to 160°C/325°F/gas 3. Line a 23x32.5cm/9x13in shallow oblong cake tin with a sheet of baking paper, snipping corners to fit.
2 Toast the hazelnuts in a small dry frying pan until light golden flecked with brown. Tip into a food processor and grind to a fine powder.
3 Blend together the cornflour, vanilla and vinegar to a smooth paste. Whisk the egg whites in a clean dry bowl until they stand in stiff peaks. Whisk in the sugar, a little at a time, adding a little of the cornflour mixture each time until all the sugar and paste is added. The meringue will be nice and thick, very white and stiff.
4 Reserve 2 tablespoons of the ground hazelnuts, then lightly fold the rest into the meringue with a metal spoon or the whisk blades until just mixed.
5 Spoon the meringue into the prepared cake tin and level the surface with the back of a spoon. Don't worry about making it too smooth as the craggy texture makes a lovely crust when baked. Sprinkle with the reserved hazelnuts.

6 Bake for about 25 minutes, until the meringue is pale golden on top and feels crisp and dryish when lightly touched. Lay a sheet of baking paper on a work surface, remove the meringue from the oven and turn it out on the paper. Peel off the lining paper and leave the meringue to cool uncovered. (It will sink slightly.)
7 Make the filling: halve the mango either side of the stone, then peel and stone it. Chop the flesh into small cubes and mix in a bowl with the sugar and orange zest. Lightly fold in the crème fraîche.
8 Spread the filling over the meringue to within 1cm/½ in of the edges. Roll up from the narrow edge, using the paper to help you (the meringue will crack slightly as it is rolled). Transfer to a serving plate and dust with icing sugar.
9 Make the sauce: peel, halve and stone the mango. Chop the flesh and whiz it in a food processor with the sugar and orange juice. Sieve if necessary, then serve with slices of roulade.

Tarte aux groseilles meringuée

You can make this delicious tart with any firm berry fruit; try blueberries for an American twist.

Serves 6

for the pastry
200g/7oz plain flour
pinch of salt
100g/3½oz caster sugar
100g/3½oz unsalted butter
2 eggs, beaten

for the filling
100g/3½oz flaked almonds
½ tsp finely grated lemon zest
2tbsp redcurrant jelly
100g/3½oz ground almonds
200g/7oz caster sugar
450g/1lb redcurrants
whites of 5 eggs
1 tbsp icing sugar

1 Make the pastry: sift the flour, salt and sugar in a thick layer on to a large chopping board or clean work surface. Cut the butter into small pieces and dot these on top. Rub the butter into the flour and sugar to form fine crumbs. Make a well in the centre, pour in the eggs and draw them into the mixture with your fingers to form a soft dough. Knead gently and shape into a ball. Wrap in cling film and chill for 30 minutes.
2 Preheat the oven to 200°C/400°F/gas 6. Roll out the pastry and use to line a 30cm/12in tart pan. Line the pastry case with foil and baking beans, and bake blind for 15 minutes, then remove the beans and foil and bake for a further 5 minutes. Remove from oven and leave to cool.
3 Reduce the oven temperature to 180°C/350°F/gas 4. In a dry non-stick frying pan, toast the

flaked almonds until pale golden, then mix in the lemon zest and redcurrant jelly. Spread the mixture evenly over the pastry base.
4 Sift the ground almonds and half the caster sugar into a bowl. Strip the redcurrants from their stems and lightly coat with the almond mixture. Arrange the redcurrants in the pastry case; set the remaining sweetened almonds aside.
5 In a clean dry, grease-free bowl, whisk the egg whites until they form stiff peaks. Sift the remaining caster sugar with the reserved sweetened ground almonds and gradually whisk into the egg whites, one tablespoon at a time, until the mixture is thick and glossy. Spoon the meringue over the redcurrants, then bake for 25-30 minutes, or until the top is pale golden and set.
6 Serve dusted with icing sugar.

More than mere trifles

The smooth charms of custards, creams and jellies

Cranberry, pear and chocolate trifle with pear crisps

The combination of tart berries, dark and white chocolates, pears and whisky turn this into a very grown-up dessert.

Serves 8

6 ripe pears
8 tbsp whisky
100g / 3½oz caster sugar, plus
    4 tbsp
450g / 1lb cranberries, defrosted if
    frozen
250g / 9oz ready-made chocolate
    sponge, cut into 1cm / ½inch slices
50g / 2oz good-quality plain
    chocolate, chopped, to decorate

**for the white chocolate
custard**

150g / 5oz good-quality white
    chocolate, chopped
400ml / 14fl oz fresh custard
300ml / ½pint double cream

for the pear crisps

2 ripe pears
100g / 3½oz sugar

1 First prepare the pear crisps: preheat the oven to 120°C / 250°F / gas ½ and line a baking sheet with baking paper. Without peeling or coring them, slice the 2 pears very thinly from top to bottom. In a frying pan, dissolve the sugar in 100ml / 3½fl oz water over a medium heat. Bring to the boil, then simmer for 2-3 minutes. Remove from the heat, add the pear slices and leave for 2 minutes, then remove with a spatula and place on a baking sheet. Place in the oven for 1½ hours until just golden, then cool on a wire rack.

2 Meanwhile, peel, core and quarter remaining 6 pears. Heat 600ml / 1pint water with a quarter of the whisky and the 100g / 3½oz sugar in a large pan, stirring, until the sugar has dissolved. Add the pears and simmer gently for 7-8 minutes until just tender. Drain and set aside to cool.

3 In a pan set over a gentle heat, cook the cranberries and the remaining 4 tablespoons of caster sugar until the berries just start to soften. Drain a spoonful on kitchen paper and reserve for decoration. Set the rest aside to cool.

4 Layer half the sponge in the bottom of a glass serving dish. Sprinkle with half the remaining whisky. Arrange half the pear quarters on top and cover with half the cranberries. Repeat layers.

5 Make the white chocolate custard: melt the white chocolate in a heatproof bowl set over a pan of simmering water (do not allow the bowl to touch the water), then leave to cool. Pour the custard into a large bowl and stir in the melted chocolate. Lightly whip the cream and fold into mixture. Pour over the trifle and chill until set.

6 To decorate, stand the pear crisps in the top of the trifle, and sprinkle over the reserved cranberries and chopped plain chocolate.

(See the picture on page 34)

Mascarpone and rum trifle

The mascarpone gives this trifle the creamy texture of a cheesecake.

Serves 6

350g / 12oz mascarpone cheese
50g / 2oz icing sugar
grated zest of 1 lemon
5 tbsp milk
5 tbsp rum
100g / 3½oz sponge fingers
150ml / ¼pint double cream
icing sugar, to dust

for the meringues

whites of 2 eggs
100g / 3½oz caster sugar

1 First make the meringues: preheat the oven to 130°C / 275°F / gas 1. Place the egg whites and sugar in a clean dry, grease-free glass or ceramic bowl and sit this over a pan of gently simmering water. Whisk (preferably with an electric whisk) until very stiff and glossy.

2 Spoon the meringue mixture into a piping bag fitted with a large star nozzle and pipe 25 small swirls of meringue on a non-stick baking sheet. Place in the oven for 50 minutes, until firm but not coloured. Increase the oven setting to 200°C / 400°F / gas 6 and bake for a further 5 minutes until golden.

3 Meanwhile, make the filling. Beat together the mascarpone cheese, icing sugar, lemon zest, and 2 tablespoons each of the milk and the rum. Cover the mixture and chill until needed.

4 Make the sponge base: mix together the remaining milk and rum. Dip the sponge fingers into the liquid and use to line the base of a glass serving dish.

5 Remove the meringues from the oven. Reserving 15 for decoration, roughly crumble the remaining meringues, fold these into the mascarpone mixture and spoon over the sponge base.

6 Whip the double cream until it forms soft peaks. Spread this on top of the mascarpone layer. Decorate the trifle with the reserved meringues and dust the top liberally with icing sugar before serving.

Fig and marsala trifle

This light Italianate trifle is quick and easy to make. Mascarpone makes a hassle-free alternative to custard.

Serves 4

200g/7oz Madeira cake, cut into
   bite-sized pieces
7tbsp Marsala or sweet sherry
8 amaretti biscuits, crushed
50g/2oz caster sugar
10 fresh figs, quartered
2tbsp icing sugar, plus extra for
   dusting
250g/9oz tub of mascarpone cheese
a little milk (optional)

1 Put the Madeira cake in a bowl and pour over 5 tablespoons of Marsala or sherry; set aside. Divide two-thirds of the crushed amaretti biscuits between 4 tall glasses. Top with the cake and set aside.

2 In a pan, gently heat the sugar and 150ml/¼ pint water, stirring until the sugar is dissolved. Bring to the boil and simmer this syrup for 4-5 minutes. Set aside 8 of the fig quarters and add the remainder to the pan. Remove from the heat and set aside to cool.

3 When the figs and syrup are cool, divide between the glasses. Beat the icing sugar into the mascarpone and stir in the remaining Marsala. If the mixture is too stiff, stir in a little milk. Spoon over the figs and chill for 30 minutes.

4 Decorate with the remaining fig quarters and amaretti biscuits. Dust with icing sugar before serving.

Raspberry syllabub trifle

This simplest variation on an ancient classic makes a great stand-by.

Serves 6

100g/3½oz sponge fingers
75g/3oz amaretti biscuits
225g/8oz fresh or frozen raspberries
225ml/8fl oz fresh orange juice (about
   4 large oranges)

for the syllabub

150ml/¼pint sherry
2tsp grated orange zest
75g/3oz caster sugar
450ml/¾pint double cream

to decorate

100g/3½oz fresh or frozen raspberries

1 Break up the sponge fingers and place in a bowl with the amaretti biscuits. Scatter over the raspberries and sprinkle with orange juice. Leave to soak for at least 1 hour, preferably 2 or 3.
2 Make the syllabub: mix together the sherry, orange zest and sugar, stirring until the sugar has dissolved. Using a wire whisk, gradually whisk in the cream, then continue whisking until the cream just holds its shape lightly.
3 Spoon the syllabub over the fruit and sponge in soft folds, then scatter over the raspberries. Chill until ready to serve.

Rhubarb and white chocolate trifle

Gary Rhodes' variation on that old favourite rhubarb and custard uses white chocolate to give it a new dimension.

675g/1½lb rhubarb
knob of butter
50-115g/2-4oz caster sugar, to taste
2tbsp orange juice
3tbsp sweet wine, sherry or brandy

for the sponge

butter for greasing
75g/2¾oz white chocolate
½tsp finely grated lemon zest
1tsp finely grated orange zest
50g/2oz plain flour
75g/2¾oz toasted hazelnuts
3 eggs, separated
75g/2¾oz caster sugar

for the custard

200ml/7fl oz milk
200ml/7fl oz double cream
1 vanilla pod (optional)
6 egg yolks
50g/2oz caster sugar
150g/5oz white chocolate, roughly
   chopped

to decorate

150ml/¼pint double cream
white and milk chocolate curls

1 First make the sponge: preheat the oven to 180ºC/350ºF/gas 4. Grease a 26x16cm/10½x6½in shallow oblong loaf pan and line it with baking paper. Roughly chop the chocolate, then whiz in a food processor until it resembles breadcrumbs. Transfer to a bowl and stir in the lemon and orange zest and flour. Blend the hazelnuts in a food processor until well ground, then stir into the chocolate mixture. Set aside.
2 In a bowl set over a pan of simmering water, whisk the egg yolks with half the sugar for about 5 minutes until the whisk leaves a trail when lifted. Off the heat, whisk for 5 minutes more until cool.
3 In a clean dry bowl, whisk the egg whites until stiff but not dry. Gradually whisk in the remaining sugar to make a meringue. Stir the hazelnut mixture into the egg yolk and sugar. Stir in 3 tablespoons of meringue to slacken the mixture, then gently fold in the rest using a large metal spoon. Pour into the loaf pan and spread evenly.
4 Bake for 25-30 minutes until risen and golden brown. Turn out on a wire rack to cool; cut in half lengthwise, then into 2.5cm/1in long fingers.
5 Make the rhubarb filling: peel any tough rhubarb stalks, then chop the rest into 1cm/½in

pieces. Melt the butter in a large pan, stir in the rhubarb and cook on a medium heat for 3 minutes. Stir in the sugar and orange juice. Cook for a further 3 minutes, stirring occasionally, until rhubarb is just tender and the juices are syrupy.
6 Drain the rhubarb in a colander over a bowl. Stir the wine, sherry or brandy into the rhubarb syrup. Arrange the sponge fingers in the base of a 1.75litre/3pint trifle dish and spoon over the syrup. Arrange the rhubarb on top of the sponge.
7 Make the custard: mix the milk and cream in a pan. Split the vanilla pod, if using, and scrape the seeds into the pan. Bring to the boil and set aside.
8 In a large bowl, whisk the egg yolks with the sugar until pale and thick. Set over a pan of simmering water and whisk in the hot milk mixture; cook, stirring constantly, until it coats the back of a spoon (about 20 minutes). Don't allow the sauce to boil or it will separate. Remove from the heat and stir in the white chocolate.
9 Cover the custard with plastic film, then chill for 2 hours until almost set. Pour it over the rhubarb and chill until set.
10 Just before serving, decorate with lightly whipped cream and chocolate curls.

Master class: making crème brûlée

Lemon crème brûlée with roasted peaches

Gary Rhodes shows you how to make the most of your brûlées.

Serves 4

3 egg yolks
finely grated zest of 2 lemons
25g/1oz caster sugar
300ml/½pint double cream
sifted icing sugar, for the topping
for the roasted peaches
40g/1½oz butter
4 large peaches
2-3tsp demerara sugar
2-3tbsp brandy (optional)

1 Preheat the oven to 180°C/350°F/gas 4. Beat together the egg yolks, lemon zest and caster sugar. In a pan, bring the double cream to the boil, then pour the hot cream into the egg mixture, whisking constantly.
2 Pour into 4 ramekins or a shallow ovenproof dish, measuring 2-3cm/½-¾ inch deep and 12.5cm/5 inches across. Set in a roasting pan and pour hot water into the pan to come three-quarters of the way up the sides of the dish(es). Bake for about 20-30 minutes until the custard is just set. Leave to cool, then chill.
3 Roast the peaches: preheat the oven to 200°C/400°F/gas 6. Heat 25g/1oz of the butter in a shallow ovenproof frying pan, then add the peaches and bubble them in the pan, turning them until uniformly golden all over. Transfer the pan to the oven and roast for about 20-30 minutes, until tender. Baste the fruit several times with the butter as it roasts.
4 Preheat the grill to high. Evenly dust the chilled custard(s) with a generous amount of icing sugar, then either grill, watching carefully, until the top caramelizes to a rich golden brown or, if making individual brûlées, use a cataplana or a salamander as shown above (1-3). For a crisper topping, repeat this step once, or even twice, more. If you have a gas-gun or blow-torch, you can use this to glaze the brûlée(s) as it gives a more even, controlled finish.
5 Carefully remove the peaches from the pan, then wipe the pan with kitchen paper. Heat the remaining butter in the pan, then return the peaches to it and sprinkle over the demerara sugar. Roll the peaches in the sugar until they start to caramelize.
6 Sprinkle over the brandy — or, if you prefer, replace with water or orange juice — and allow to bubble up to form a sauce.
7 To serve, place a roasted peach on each serving plate, trickle over a little of the sauce and place a lemon crème brûlée to the side, or spoon some from the larger dish.

Orange cheesecake brûlée with orange sauce

Given a brûlée topping, this easy cheesecake becomes an impressive desserts.

Serves 8

200g/7oz caster sugar
thinly pared rind and juice of 2
    oranges
1 Madeira cake, about 250g/9oz in
    weight, cut into thin slices
4tbsp Cointreau or other orange-
    flavoured liqueur
250g/9oz quark cheese
250g/9oz mascarpone cheese
2tsp vanilla essence
300ml/½ pint double cream
100g/3½oz icing sugar

1 In a heavy-based pan over a gently heat, dissolve 175g/6oz of the sugar in 150ml/¼ pint water. Bring to the boil and cook without stirring for 3 minutes until syrupy. Cut the orange rind into strips, add to the pan and cook for 1 minute.
2 Line the base of a 23cm/9in spring-release or loose-bottomed cake pan with the cake slices, trimming them so they fit in an even layer. Spoon over 4 tablespoons of the orange syrup.
3 Heat the remaining syrup until it forms a golden caramel, then immerse the base of the pan in cold water to prevent further cooking. Stir in the orange juice and liqueur, taking care as it may splatter, and return to the heat, stirring until it forms a smooth caramel. Set aside to cool.
4 In a bowl, beat together the quark, mascarpone, remaining sugar and vanilla. Whip the cream until lightly thickened, then fold it into the mixture. Spoon over the sponge and level the surface.
5 Preheat the grill to high. Dust the cheesecake with the icing sugar and grill until just beginning to colour. Chill for at least 2 hours or until firm.
6 Remove the cheesecake from the cake pan. Holding one end with an oven glove, heat a long flat skewer over the hob (gas or electric) until it starts to glow, then quickly and lightly scorch parallel lines across the cheesecake to caramelize the icing sugar. Reheat the skewer as necessary. Chill, then serve with the orange sauce.

Note:
The skewer will be irretrievably blackened so keep one especially for searing – try it on millefeuilles, gâteaux and other sugar-dusted desserts.

The scorching principle used to such effect on the Orange cheesecake brûlée opposite can transform any flat-topped dessert dusted with icing sugar.

Instant fruit brûlée

This is the cheat's way to brûlées – without any grilling or hot irons – and it works for most mixtures of fruit.

Serves 6

6 passion fruit
2 large ripe mangoes, peeled, stoned
and cut into thin slices
150g/5oz blueberries
200g/7oz caster sugar, plus 1tbsp
450ml/¾ pint double cream
2tbsp icing sugar

1 Scoop out the seeds from the passion fruit into a glass serving dish and toss with the mangoes, blueberries and the 1 tablespoon of caster sugar.
2 In a bowl, whip the cream together with the icing sugar until it just holds its shape. Spoon the cream over the fruits in the serving dish, piling it up in the centre. Chill while you prepare the syrup.
3 In a small heavy-based pan, gently heat the 200g/7oz caster sugar with 6 tablespoons of water until the sugar dissolves. Bring to the boil and cook until the syrup turns a mid-golden caramel colour. (Overcooked caramel is bitter; stop cooking the moment it turns a deep golden colour — it also starts to smell marvellous at this point.) Leave to stand for 2 minutes, then drizzle the caramel slowly over the cream mountain so it runs down in little streams.
4 Serve immediately or leave at room temperature for about 1 hour until the caramel starts to soften.

Light lemon and nutmeg brûlée

Inspired by the light brûlées of Spain, this cream-free version is deliciously scented — an extra surprise when you crunch through the topping.

Serves 4

2 lemons
500ml/18fl oz full-fat milk
1 cinnamon stick
freshly grated nutmeg
4 egg yolks
115g/4oz caster sugar
2tbsp cornflour

1 Pare strips of rind from the lemons and put them in a pan with the milk, cinnamon and a sprinkling of grated nutmeg. Bring just to the boil, then reduce the heat and simmer very gently for 10 minutes.

2 In a heatproof bowl, whisk together the egg yolks and 55g/2oz of the sugar until foamy, then stir in the cornflour. Strain the milk over the egg mixture, stirring constantly, then return to the pan and cook over a gentle heat, stirring until thickened and smooth. Simmer gently for 5 minutes.

3 Pour the mixture into 4 shallow flameproof dishes. Allow to cool and then chill for at least 4 hours, or preferably overnight, until they are lightly set.

4 Preheat the grill to high. Sprinkle the dishes with the remaining sugar — you may need a little extra if the dishes are particularly shallow and wide. Place under the hot grill or use a gas-gun, blow-torch, cataplana or salamander (see page 42) to caramelize the tops. Serve or chill until you are ready to serve.

Tiramisu cheesecake

Coffee, chocolate and nuts give this cheesecake bags of Italian style.

Serves 6

for the base
85g/3oz butter, plus more for the pan
175g/6oz ginger biscuits, crushed
50g/2oz pecans, finely chopped

for the filling
175g/6oz plain chocolate
150ml/¼pint double cream
225g/8oz mascarpone cheese
1tbsp cold strong black coffee
50g/2oz caster sugar

to decorate
25g/1oz plain chocolate
225g/8oz mascarpone cheese
100g/3½oz thick Greek yoghurt
25g/1oz pecans, roughly chopped
cocoa, for sprinkling

1 Make the base: melt the butter in a pan and stir in the crushed biscuits and pecans. Press into the base of a lightly greased 17.5cm/7in round fluted flan pan. Chill.

2 Make the filling: melt the chocolate in a bowl set over a pan of simmering water; allow to cool slightly. Whip the cream until stiff. Beat the mascarpone in a bowl with the coffee, sugar and chocolate. Gently fold in the cream. Pour into the flan pan and smooth the top. Chill until firm.

3 Meanwhile, melt the chocolate for decoration in a bowl over a pan of simmering water; allow to cool.

4 Transfer the cheesecake to a serving plate. Mix together the mascarpone and yoghurt and swirl over the top of the cheesecake. Drizzle over the chocolate and sprinkle liberally with the pecans and cocoa.

Chocolate praline brûlées

Although looking and tasting quite sensational, these brûlées are deceptively easy to make.

Serves 6

150ml/¼pint double cream
250g/9oz good-quality plain
    chocolate, broken into pieces
4tbsp brandy
250g/9oz fromage frais
115g/4oz caster sugar
25g/1oz flaked almonds, lightly
    toasted

1 In a pan, bring the cream just to the boil, then remove from the heat and add the chocolate, stirring frequently until the chocolate has melted to make a smooth glossy sauce. Stir in the brandy, fromage frais and 25g/1oz of the sugar, then pour the mixture into 6 small ramekins or dessert pots and scatter over the almonds.

2 In a small heavy-based pan, gently heat the remaining sugar with 3 tablespoons of water until the sugar has dissolved. Bring to the boil, then boil rapidly for about 5 minutes until the syrup has turned a pale caramel colour. Immerse the base of the pan in cold water to prevent further cooking (it will hiss).

3 Using a teaspoon, drizzle the syrup in a thin stream over the almonds — don't drizzle over too much or it will be thick and brittle. It will set almost instantly but, if allowed to stand, the caramel slowly and deliciously softens.

45

Peach and honeycomb fool

Turn peaches into an extra-delicious treat with the easiest of treatments.

Serves 4

400g/14oz fromage frais
6 peaches, peeled and stoned
80g honeycomb or Crunchie bar,
   roughly crushed
sprigs of mint or lemon balm,
   to decorate

1 Put the fromage frais into a bowl. Place the peaches in a food processor and process until smooth. Lightly fold the purée and most of the honeycomb into the fromage frais.
2 Spoon the mixture into individual glasses and decorate with the remaining honeycomb and sprigs of mint or lemon balm. Serve immediately.

Almond palmiers with nectarine cream

Make the palmiers in advance; they'll keep in an airtight tin for a week, or in the freezer for up to three months, but re-crisp for a few minutes in a moderate oven before using.

Serves 8

450g/1lb puff pastry, defrosted if
   frozen
450g/1lb white marzipan
200ml/7fl oz crème fraîche
icing sugar, for dusting
lime wedges, to serve
mint sprigs, to decorate
for the Nectarine Compote
350g/12oz nectarines, skinned,
   stoned and roughly chopped
4tbsp apple juice
50g/2oz caster sugar

1 First make the nectarine compote: put the prepared nectarines in a pan and pour over the apple juice and sugar. Leave to stand for 15 minutes. Then cook over a gentle heat until the nectarines have softened but not collapsed. Allow to cool.
2 Preheat the oven to 200°C/400°F/gas 6. On a lightly floured surface, roll out the pastry to a 30x24cm/12x9.5in rectangle. Set aside. On a surface dusted with icing sugar, roll out the marzipan to the same size. Lift the marzipan on top of the pastry and press down lightly with a rolling pin.
3 Fold the long sides in to the centre, leaving a small gap between them, then fold each piece in half to the middle again. Cut into 16 slices.
4 Place one palmier between two pieces of plastic film and roll out to 10x6cm/4x2.5 inches. Remove the film. Repeat with the remaining palmiers and place them, well spaced, on baking sheets lined with non-stick baking paper. Bake for 6-8 minutes, until risen and crisp. Allow to cool on a wire rack.
5 Spoon the crème fraîche and nectarine compote over 8 of the palmiers. Top with the remaining palmiers and dust with icing sugar.
6 Serve with fresh lime wedges and decorated with sprigs of fresh mint.

Coconut cream with Malibu fruits

Give a miscellany of summer fruit the totally tropical treatment.

Serves 8-10

for the coconut cream
8 sheets of fine-leaf gelatine
4tbsp Malibu or other rum- or fruit-
 based liqueur
500g/1lb 1½oz tub of vanilla
 fromage frais
600ml/1pint coconut cream
115g/4oz caster sugar
600ml/1pint whipping cream, lightly
 whipped

for the fruits
2 ripe papayas, peeled, deseeded
 and sliced
450g/1lb strawberries, hulled and
 halved
225g/8oz raspberries
225g/8oz blueberries
4tbsp caster sugar
4tbsp Malibu or other rum- or fruit-
 based liqueur
strawberry leaves or fresh mint, to
 decorate

1 Break the gelatine into a heatproof bowl and measure in 4 tablespoons of water and the liqueur. Set aside to soak for 5 minutes. Place the bowl over a pan of simmering water, stirring the mixture occasionally until the gelatine has dissolved.

2 In a separate bowl, beat together the fromage frais, coconut cream and sugar. Stir in the gelatine mixture, then fold in the cream. Pour into a large glass serving bowl, cover with plastic film and chill until ready to serve.

3 Place the fruits in a bowl, sprinkle over the sugar and drizzle over the liqueur. Set aside at room temperature.

4 Just before serving, pile the fruits over the coconut cream and decorate with strawberry leaves or fresh mint.

Fast and Foolish

Spangled berry cream

Serves 4

Bring juice of 1 orange and 2 tablespoons redcurrant jelly to the boil in a small pan and boil rapidly for 2-3 minutes until thickened. Stir in 350g / 12 oz mixed berries, such as raspberries, strawberries, blueberries and redcurrants, and remove from heat. Using a slotted spoon, transfer 50g / 2oz of berries to a small bowl. Tip rest into a serving dish and leave to cool a little. Whip 150ml / 1/4 pint whipping cream to soft peaks, then fold in 150g / 5oz thick Greek yoghurt and grated zest from orange. Sprinkle 10 crushed amaretti biscuits over berry mixture and swirl cream and yoghurt on top. Spoon over reserved berries.

Meanwhile, place 50g / 2oz caster sugar in a small pan with 1 tablespoon of cold water. Heat gently until sugar has completely dissolved, then increase heat and boil rapidly, without stirring, until a light golden caramel. Remove from heat, allow to cool for 1 minute, then quickly drizzle caramel strands on top of dessert. Chill until ready to serve.

Summer fruit sabayon

Serves 4

Place 2 beaten egg yolks and 50g / 2oz caster sugar in a heatproof bowl and beat until well combined. Add grated zest of 1/2 lemon and 150ml / 1/4 pint dry white wine, then set bowl over a pan of simmering water (do not allow bowl to touch water). Continue beating until sabayon is smooth and thick. Gradually stir in 4 tablespoons of single cream and whisk for 1 minute until well combined. Arrange 450g / 1lb mixed summer fruit, such as blueberries, raspberries, stoned cherries, grapes and apricot wedges, in a shallow ovenproof dish, pour over the sabayon and place under a hot grill until golden. Serve at once.

Quick apricot fool

Serves 4-6

Drain two 400g/14oz cans of apricot halves in natural juice. Slice 2 of the apricot halves and set these
aside. Purée the rest in a blender or food processor
with 3 tablespoons clear honey and the grated zest
and juice of 1 lime until smooth. Transfer to a mixing
bowl. Gently fold in 350ml/12fl oz ready-made custard and 150 ml/¹/₄ pint double cream, whipped.
Serve decorated with the reserved apricot slices and
some herb sprigs or pared lime rind cut into fine juli-
enne strips.

Highland flummery

Serves 6

Melt 15g/¹/₂oz butter in a frying pan, add 100g/
3¹/₂oz porridge oats and stir-fry for 3-4 minutes until
toasted. Add 1 tablespoon light muscovado sugar and
remove from the heat. Whip 300ml/¹/₂ pint whipping
cream until it just holds its shape and gradually
whisk in 3 tablespoons of heather honey.
4 tablespoons of Drambuie and the juice of 1 small
lime. Reserve 1 tablespoon of the oat mixture and
halve the remainder. Divide the first half between 6
glasses and top with half the cream. Repeat. Sprinkle
the reserved oat mixture on top. Decorate with
raspberries and blueberries, grated lime zest and
mint leaves.

Currants in red wine jelly

Banish the nursery associations of jelly with this very unusual treatment that suits the most grown-up of tables.

Serves 6

600ml/1pint red wine
175g/6oz caster sugar
1 orange
675g/1½lb mixed redcurrants and
 blackcurrants
15g/½oz powdered gelatine
6 fresh mint leaves

1 Pour the red wine and sugar into a pan. Pare the rind from the orange, taking care not to include any pith. Squeeze the juice, then add the rind and the juice to the pan with 150ml/¼ pint water. Bring to the boil, then simmer for 15 minutes.
2 Strain into a jug, then return the juice to the pan. Add the currants and cook gently for 2 minutes. Strain, then boil briefly. Remove from the heat and stir in the gelatine until dissolved.

3 Leave the syrup to cool, then chill until it is just starting to set; stir in the mixed currants. Rinse six 150ml/¼ pint moulds or ramekins with cold water. Place a mint leaf in the base of each mould, then carefully spoon in the jelly. Set the moulds on a tray or plate and chill for 3 hours or overnight until they are set.
4 Briefly dip the moulds in hot water, turn out on to small plates and serve.

White chocolate and blueberry jelly cheesecake

Toasted nut base, creamy white chocolate filling and joyful fruit jelly topping make this everyone's favourite.

Serves 8-10

for the base
175g/6oz toasted hazelnuts
50g/2oz icing sugar
50g/2oz butter, melted, plus more for
 the pan

for the filling
400g/14oz white chocolate, broken
 into pieces
two 500g/1lb 1½oz tubs of
 fromage frais
11g sachet of powdered gelatine

for the jelly topping
11g sachet of powdered gelatine
350g/12oz blueberries
50g/2oz caster sugar
juice of ½ lemon

1 Process the hazelnuts and icing sugar in a food processor or blender until the nuts are finely chopped. Pour in the melted butter and process again. Press the mixture firmly on the base of a lightly buttered 23cm/9in loose-bottomed flan pan and chill.
2 Make the filling: melt the chocolate in a bowl set over a pan of gently simmering water, stirring until smooth. Remove from the heat; beat in the fromage frais.
3 Sprinkle the gelatine over 5 tablespoons of boiling water in a small bowl, then stir until dissolved and translucent. Stir into the fromage frais mixture, pour over the hazelnut base and chill.
4 Meanwhile, make the jelly topping: sprinkle the gelatine over 4 tablespoons of cold water in a small bowl and set aside to soak.
5 In a pan, heat half the blueberries, the sugar, lemon juice and 300ml/½pint of water, until the liquid is boiling and purple in colour. Allow to cool slightly, stir in the soaked gelatine and remaining berries, remove from the heat and cool.
6 When the jelly mixture has cooled, spoon it over the top of the cheesecake and return to the fridge for about 3 hours until set.
7 To serve, carefully run a wet knife round the top of the cheesecake to loosen the jelly before removing from the tin.

Winning the Toss

A bewitching battery of pancakes, crêpes and waffles

Master class: making pancakes

Basic pancakes

Makes 10-12

100g/3½oz plain flour
1 egg, plus 1 egg yolk
300ml/½ pint semi-skimmed milk
1tbsp sunflower oil, plus extra for frying

1 Sift the flour into a bowl(1). Make a well in the centre, and add the egg, egg yolk and half the milk (2).

2 Using a wooden spoon or balloon whisk, beat the eggs and milk together, incorporating the flour at the same time (3). When the mixture starts to thicken, gradually add the remaining milk (4) until the consistency is that of thin cream (make sure there are no lumps). Beat in the oil. Cover and leave for 30 minutes.

3 Preheat the oven to 110°C/230°F/gas ¼ (to keep the cooked pancakes warm). Heat a little oil in an 17.5cm/7in heavy-based crêpe or frying pan. Pour in enough batter (either from a jug or using a ladle) to cover the base of the pan thinly (5), swirling the batter around the pan to form an even layer. Cook for 1 minute or so until small holes start to appear in the pancake.

4 Using a palette knife, carefully turn the pancake over (6) and cook for 1 minute. Remove from the pan. Repeat this process until you have used all the batter. As you make the pancakes, stack them on a plate, separating them with greaseproof paper. Keep them warm, wrapped in foil in the low oven.

Notes:
* If the batter is left to stand, it produces better pancakes. However, you may need to stir in a little extra milk as it tends to thicken on standing.
* You can add a little caster sugar to the batter to sweeten it if you wish, or a good pinch of salt if you want to make pancakes with a savoury filling.

Lace pancakes with raspberry and honey cream

Phil Vickery's elegant lace pancakes give a new dimension to a classic concept.

Serves 6

2 eggs
100g/3½oz plain flour
pinch of salt
2 pinches of sugar
300ml/½ pint full-fat milk
15g/½oz butter, melted
300ml/½ pint double cream
1-2tsp clear honey, to taste
225g/8oz fresh raspberries
vegetable oil, for frying
icing sugar, for dusting

1 In a bowl, whisk together the eggs, flour, salt and sugar until combined, then whisk in the milk until you have a smooth batter. Whisk in the melted butter, then pass the batter through a fine sieve.
2 Half whip the cream and sweeten with the honey to taste. Fold in the raspberries and chill.
3 Heat a few drops of oil in a non-stick frying pan until hot. Pour the batter into a piping bag fitted with a very fine nozzle. Starting in the centre of the pan, pipe a thin stream of batter and continue piping around, then across the pan to form a spider's web pattern with a diameter of about 13cm/5¼in. Cook until set, then turn over and cook for a few minutes more until brown and crisp; remove and leave to cool. Repeat with the remaining batter to make 12 pancakes; keep warm.
4 Place a pancake on each plate, spoon some of the raspberry and honey cream in the centre and top with another pancake. Lightly dust with icing sugar and serve immediately.

Lacy peach crêpes

Serves 4

3 peaches, halved and stoned
25g/1oz icing sugar
2tbsp crème de cassis
2tbsp fresh orange juice
50g/2oz plain flour
1 egg
150ml/¼ pint milk
oil, for frying
icing sugar, for dusting
whipped cream or ice cream, to serve

1 Slice each peach into eight, then mix with the icing sugar, liqueur and orange juice and leave to macerate while you make the crêpes.
2 Sift the flour into a bowl, make a well in the centre and add the egg. Gradually beat in the milk to form a smooth batter which has the consistency of single cream.
3 Heat 1 teaspoon of oil in an 17.5cm/7in non-stick frying pan. Using a large spoon, drizzle about 2 tablespoons of batter over the frying pan to give a lacy effect. (Don't tilt the pan or the batter will run together.) Cook for 2 minutes, then flip and cook the other side for 1-2 minutes until golden.

4 Repeat with the remaining batter to make 8. Fill the crêpes with the peach mixture and fold them in half. Dust with icing sugar and serve with whipped cream or ice cream.

Apple and cinnamon sugar crêpes

Serves 4

2tbsp caster sugar
¼tsp ground cinnamon
50g/2oz plain flour
1 egg
150ml/¼ pint milk
oil, for frying
2 red apples, sliced
115g/4oz sultanas
icing sugar, for dusting
crème fraîche or ice cream, to serve

1 In a bowl, mix the sugar and cinnamon together.
2 Sift the flour into a bowl, make a well in the centre and add the egg. Gradually beat in the milk to form a smooth batter which has the consistency of single cream.
3 Heat 1 teaspoon of oil in an 17.5cm/7in non-stick frying pan. Using a large spoon, drizzle about 2 tablespoons of batter over the frying pan to give a lacy effect. (Take care not to tilt the pan or the batter will run together.) Cook for 2 minutes, then flip over and cook the other side for 1-2 minutes until golden.

4 Repeat with the remaining batter to make 8.
5 Sprinkle each crêpe with the cinnamon sugar, then arrange the apple slices and sultanas on top. Fold them in half, or into quarters. Dust with icing sugar and serve with crème fraîche or ice cream.

Master class: crêpes Suzettes

Crêpes Suzettes

The showiest restaurant dessert of all time, crêpes Suzettes are back in vogue again. You can do it at home, with or without the theatricality.

Serves 4

for the crêpes
100g/3½oz plain flour
25g/1oz caster sugar
grated zest of 1 orange
1 egg
300ml/½ pint milk
25g/1oz butter, melted, plus extra for frying

for the sauce
juice of 2 oranges
juice and grated zest of 1 lemon
3tbsp Cointreau or Grand Marnier
75g/2¾oz caster sugar
100g/3½oz butter
2tbsp brandy or rum

1 Make the pancakes: in a bowl, mix together the flour, sugar and orange zest. Make a well in the centre and drop in the egg, unbeaten. Start to beat the egg, adding half the milk in a steady stream and gradually pulling the flour into the egg mixture. Once all the flour has been incorporated, beat vigorously for 2-3 minutes until the batter is smooth. Stir in the remaining milk and the melted butter to make a smooth, shiny batter that just coats the back of a wooden spoon.

2 In a 20cm / 8in frying pan or pancake pan (preferably non-stick), heat a little butter, then ladle in a little batter, swirling the pan to coat the base as thinly as you can.

3 When the batter turns a darker yellow and feels firm, use a palette knife to life up the edges, then slide the knife under the pancake, flip and cook for 1-2 minutes. Transfer to a plate, cover with foil to keep warm and make the remaining pancakes — this quantity of batter should make about 8.

4 Make the sauce: in a bowl, mix together the orange and lemon juices, the lemon zest and the orange liqueur. In a heavy-based frying pan, gently heat the sugar and 1 tablespoon of the citrus mixture, tilting the pan occasionally, until the sugar has melted and turned a toffee colour.

5 Cut the butter into small cubes and add to the sugar in the pan (1). Swirl it into the pan until it has melted into the sauce (2). Pour the remaining citrus mixture into the pan (3) and stir well until the caramel has completely dissolved and you have a glossy sauce.

6 Fold each pancake into quarters, then slide these into the pan (4), basting each one with caramel as it is added. Heat through for about 1 minute. When the juices are bubbling, quickly pour on the brandy or rum and ignite. Serve immediately.

Notes:
* Dissolving sugar is a tricky business. Be patient and don't be tempted to stir in the sugar as it can crystallize if you fiddle with it. Use a heavy-based pan, preferably one that distributes the heat evenly. The sugar will start to dissolve in one place, so when this happens, tilt the pan to spread the caramel on to the undissolved sugar. Don't worry if the caramel forms lumps when the citrus mixture is added; just bubble it up and it will dissolve back into the sauce.
* The pancakes can be made any time on the day that you are going to serve them as they reheat well in the sauce, which can also be made any time on the day. Don't, however, put the pancakes into the sauce until just before serving or they'll go grey and limp.

American breakfast pancakes

These thick, almost juicy, pancakes from Michael Barry get a spicy sweetness from the maple syrup.

Makes 16

225g/8oz self-raising flour
1tsp baking powder
25g/1oz caster sugar
pinch of salt
2 eggs
300ml/½ pint milk or equal parts
    milk and water
1tbsp melted butter
olive oil, for frying
more cold butter and maple syrup, to
    serve

1 Mix together all the dry ingredients. Beat the eggs with the milk, add the melted butter and pour over the dry ingredients, whisking well. Don't mix them in a food processor as it makes the pancakes a little rubbery.
2 Leave the batter to stand for 5 minutes while you heat a big pan, preferably about 30cm/12in wide. Lightly grease the pan with oil each time before using it. Stir the batter before making each pancake. Using a ladle, take about 2 tablespoons of batter and pour it into a quarter of the pan, wait until it settles before adding more (three or four at a time is ideal — each one should be about 10cm/4in wide).

3 The pancakes will bubble up, becoming quite thick (up to 1cm/½in). When they are browned on one side (after about 1½ minutes), flip them over with a fish slice and press down lightly. Cook for 1 more minute. Serve with a knob of butter and maple syrup.

Variation:
The Americans might serve these with crispy bacon – and lashings of maple syrup – for breakfast, but they also suit ice cream or fruit purées as accompaniments when served as a sweet course. Try flavouring the batter with a scant teaspoon of cinnamon.

American breakfast pancakes, opposite, dripping with maple syrup, can make a buffet-table dessert to accompany fruit or fruit compotes.

Lemony crêpes

Serves 4

100g/3½oz plain flour
pinch of salt
1 egg, beaten
300ml/½ pint milk
vegetable oil, for frying
50g/2oz butter
25g/1oz caster sugar
pared rind and juice of 1 orange
100g/3½oz lemon curd
2tbsp brandy (optional)

1 Sift the flour and salt into a bowl, add the egg and beat well. Gradually beat in the milk to make a smooth batter.
2 Heat a little of the oil in a frying pan and pour in enough batter to coat the base of the pan thinly. Cook for 1-2 minutes, turn and cook until golden, then transfer to a plate. Repeat with the remaining batter to make 8 pancakes.
3 Melt the butter in the pan. Remove from the heat and add the sugar, orange rind and juice; heat gently to dissolve the sugar.
4 Spread the lemon curd on the pancakes, then fold each pancake in half and then in half again to form a fan shape.

5 Place the pancakes in the pan in overlapping lines and heat gently for 1-2 minutes. Warm the brandy, if using it, then pour it over the pancakes and carefully set alight. Shake and serve.

Variation:
Use a good-quality marmalade instead of the lemon curd and replace the orange with a lemon.

Waffles with date and orange compote

Serves 4

100ml/3½fl oz port
100g/3½oz caster sugar
finely pared rind and juice of 2 limes
2 oranges, segmented
125g/4½oz fresh dates, halved and
  stoned
50g/2oz pecan nuts
4 doughnut waffles, warmed
icing sugar, for dusting

1 Place the port, caster sugar and lime rind and juice in a pan, bring to the boil and simmer, stirring occasionally, for 5 minutes until the mixture is syrupy.
2 Stir in the oranges and dates and warm through for 2-3 minutes. Stir in the pecan nuts.
3 Dust the warmed waffles with icing sugar and serve with the compote.

Variation:
Replace the pecans with toasted whole or slivered almonds.

Buttermilk pancakes with apple and pecan maple syrup

Serves 4

100g/3½oz plain flour
2tsp baking powder
½tsp bicarbonate of soda
1tbsp caster sugar
½tsp salt
2 eggs, separated
250ml/8fl oz buttermilk
25g/1oz butter, melted, plus more
  for frying
**for the apple, pecan and
maple syrup topping**
2 large eating apples
25g/1oz butter
250ml/8fl oz maple syrup
100g/3½oz pecan nuts

1 Sift the flour, baking powder, bicarbonate of soda, sugar and salt into a bowl. Mix together the egg yolks, buttermilk and melted butter and whisk into the flour mixture until the batter is thick and smooth (don't over-beat). Whisk the egg whites until stiff, then carefully fold them into the batter.
2 Prepare the topping: peel, core and quarter the apples, then slice each apple quarter into 4 pieces. Heat the butter in a large frying pan and cook the apple slices until coloured and softened. Meanwhile, in another pan, heat the maple syrup with the pecan nuts for 3-4 minutes until thickened.
3 Make the pancakes: heat a large frying pan, preferably non-stick, and brush lightly with melted butter. Drop large spoonfuls of batter (about 3 tablespoons — there should be enough batter for 8-9 pancakes) into the pan. When bubbles appear on the surface, flip the pancake over and cook until browned. Transfer to a plate and keep warm.

4 Place 4 apple slices on each buttermilk pancake and cover with a spoonful of the maple syrup. Top with a second pancake, 4 more apple slices and a large spoonful of the maple syrup. Repeat with the remaining ingredients to make 3 more stacks of pancakes. Serve at once.

Variation:
For a blueberry and cinnamon topping, place 225g/8oz fresh or frozen blueberries in a pan with 50g/2oz demerara sugar and 50ml/2fl oz water and simmer gently until the blueberries have softened — this takes about 2 minutes for fresh and 5 for frozen. Blend 2 teaspoons of cornflour with 1 tablespoon of water to a smooth paste and stir into the blueberry sauce with a teaspoon of ground cinnamon. Bring to the boil and simmer until thickened. Serve hot or cold with the buttermilk pancakes.

The Upper Crust

The ultimate temptation of tarts, pies and pastries

Torta di mandorle e pere (Almond and pear tart)

Serves 10

for the pastry
225g/8oz plain flour
75g/2¾oz caster sugar
pinch of salt
zest of 1 orange
140g/5oz unsalted butter, at room
  temperature
1tbsp dark rum
3tbsp apricot conserve

for the filling
75g/2¾oz butter
75g/2¾oz caster sugar
75g/2¾oz ground almonds
1 large egg, beaten
1tbsp dark rum
4 ripe pears, such as Rocha, peeled,
  halved and cored
3-4tbsp flaked almonds
beaten egg, for glazing
icing sugar, for dusting
lightly whipped double cream or
  crème fraîche, to serve

1 Make the pastry: put the flour, sugar and salt in a bowl. Use a zester or grater to remove the zest from the orange and add to the flour. Make a well in the centre. Roughly break up the butter with your fingers and add it to the flour. Using a round-bladed knife, cut the butter into the flour, then shake the bowl so that any larger pieces come to the surface. Keep cutting until all the butter is in tiny pieces; work the mixture with your hands to break it up even more. Add the rum and about 3 tablespoons of cold water, then lightly work together to make a ball, adding a little more water if it feels dry. Wipe the pastry round the bowl to collect the bits. It should be slightly damp, never dry. Wrap in plastic film and chill for 15 minutes.
2 Preheat the oven to 200°C/400°F/gas 6. Cut off 100g/3½oz of the dough for the lattice top, wrap and return to the fridge. Press the rest into a flat even ball, put it in the centre of a 2.5cm/1in deep 23cm/9in flan pan and press evenly over the bottom of pan with the fingers, then work pastry up the sides with the thumbs. If the pastry feels thick at the sides, continue to press to thin it, letting the excess fall over the edge (trim off later). Cover with plastic film and chill for 30 minutes.

3 Prick the pastry base lightly with a fork, then line with greaseproof paper and fill with baking beans. Bake for 12-15 minutes until the pastry no longer looks raw. Remove the paper and beans, then bake for 10-12 minutes more until pale golden. Spread the apricot conserve over the pastry base while warm; leave to cool.
4 Make the filling: beat the butter and sugar together until pale and creamy. Beat in the ground almonds, egg and rum. Arrange the pears over the bottom of the cooled pastry case. Spoon the ground almond mixture over the top so you can still see some of the pears. Sprinkle over the flaked almonds.
5 Roll out the reserved pastry and cut into six 1cm/½in wide strips (use a fluted pastry wheel or sharp knife). Weave the strips over the pears to make a wide lattice. Brush the strips with beaten egg and return tart to the oven for 25-30 minutes until filling is set and the tart is golden. Dust with icing sugar while still warm and serve warm or cold with lightly whipped double cream or crème fraîche.

(See the picture on page 64)

Crostata di fichi e limoni (Fig and lemon tart)

This tart is based on an ancient Italian recipe which involves boiling whole lemons, then slicing them thinly with their skins into the tart shell before topping with figs. This version is not quite so sharp, having a smooth and creamy lemon base, and the figs snuggle in an apricot and lemon glaze.

Serves 10

for the pastry
175g/6oz plain flour
75g/2¾oz caster sugar
75g/2¾oz unsalted butter, at room
  temperature
1 egg
1tsp vanilla essence
pinch of salt

1 Make the pastry: pile the flour on a work surface, then make a large wide crater in the middle and tip in the sugar. Roughly line the crater with the sugar. Pinch the butter into pieces and arrange these around the sugar. Break the egg into the centre, then add the vanilla and a pinch of salt. Using a fork, break up the egg and start to bring in the dry ingredients, breaking up the butter as you go. Gather all the ingredients together using only your fingertips. As you feel the

butter breaking down, rub it in lightly until the dough feels damper and there are no lumps of butter left — just speckles. Form the dough into a ball, gathering up any dry bits around the edge. Knead the dough lightly until smooth, then wrap in plastic film and chill for 15 minutes.
2 Make the filling: put the egg and sugar in a heatproof bowl and whisk until frothy. Whisk in the flour and 1 tablespoon of the milk. Heat the remaining milk in a pan, then pour, stirring, on to

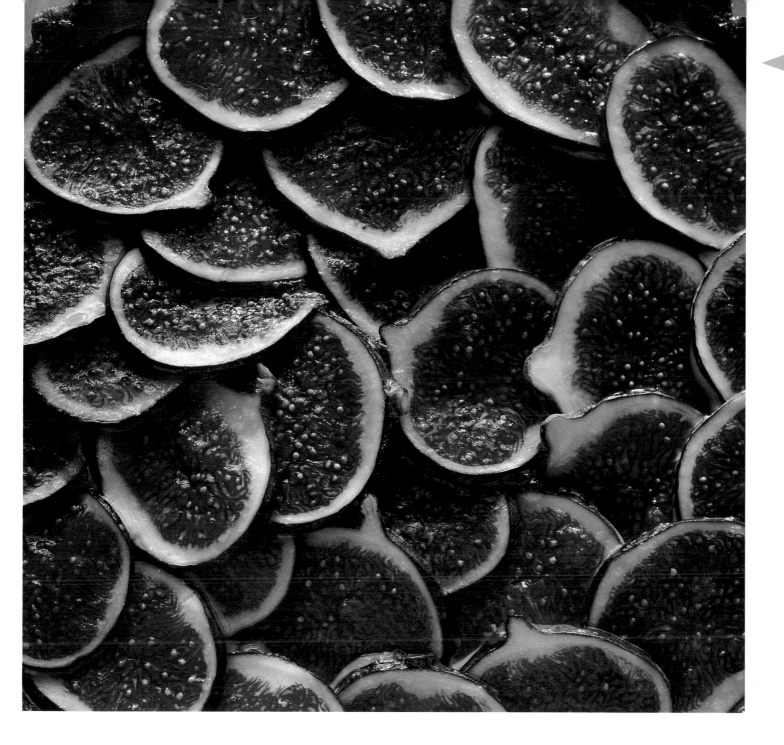

for the filling

1 egg

50g/2oz caster sugar

45g/1½oz plain flour

300ml/½ pint milk

25g/1oz butter, diced

a few drops of vanilla essence

grated zest and juice of 1 lemon

200ml/7fl oz carton of crème fraîche

5 ripe figs

4tbsp apricot conserve

lightly whipped double cream, to
serve

the egg mixture. Return the mixture to the pan and cook over a medium heat, stirring until the custard is thickened and smooth — do not boil! Remove from the heat and beat in the butter, vanilla and lemon zest. Cover with greaseproof paper and leave to cool. When cold, beat in the crème fraîche.

3 Preheat the oven to 200°C/400°F/gas 6. Roll out the pastry on a lightly floured surface and use to line a 2.5cm/1in deep 23cm/9in flan pan. (Lay the pastry over a rolling pin, then carefully unroll it into the pan.) Ease the pastry into the edges of the pan with your knuckles. Trim the

edges by running the rolling pin over the pan. Prick the pastry base lightly with a fork, then line with greaseproof paper and fill with baking beans or dried beans. Cook for 12-15 minutes, then remove the paper and beans. Bake for 10-12 minutes more until pale golden; allow to cool. Spoon in the filling and chill for 1 hour until softly set; it should be just firm enough to slice.

4 Thinly slice the figs down from the stalk and arrange on top of the filling. In a small pan, heat the lemon juice and apricot conserve, then sieve it. Brush this glaze over the figs and pastry edges. Serve the tart with lightly whipped double cream.

Master class: making cheesecake

Yorkshire curd tart

Serves 6

for the pastry
200g/7oz plain flour
100g/3½oz butter, cut into small pieces,
    plus extra for greasing
25g/1oz caster sugar
for the filling
85g/3oz caster sugar
85g/3oz softened butter
500g/1lb 2oz curd or medium-fat soft cheese
grated zest and juice of 1 lemon
3 eggs, beaten
50g/2oz currants or seedless raisins
freshly grated nutmeg, for sprinkling
icing sugar, for dusting

1 Make the pastry: preheat the oven to 200°C/400°F/gas 6 and grease a 23cm/9in loose-bottomed flan pan and set on a baking sheet. Put the flour into a bowl and rub in the butter with your fingertips until the mixture has the consistency of fine bread-crumbs (1). Stir in the sugar, then add about 2 or 3 tablespoons of cold water and mix to a firm dough.
2 Knead the dough briefly on a floured surface, then roll out to a 27.5cm/11in round, using short sharp strokes and giving the dough a quarter turn after each rolling. Flip the pastry over the rolling pin, then lift carefully on to the flan pan. Ease the pastry into the bottom and sides of the pan with your fingers, allowing it to flop over the top. Run the rolling pin over the top to trim the pastry to a neat edge (3). Line the pastry case with greaseproof paper and fill with baking beans, dried beans or rice. Bake for 15 minutes, then remove the paper and beans and bake for a further 5 minutes. Reduce the oven setting to 180°C/350°F/gas 4.
3 Make the filling: in a bowl, beat together the sugar and butter for about 5 minutes until pale and light (2). Stir in the cheese and lemon zest, making sure the mixture is well blended. Gradually beat in the lemon juice, followed by the eggs, a little at a time.
4 Stir in the dried fruit, then pour the mixture into the pastry case (4). Bake for 30-35 minutes until the filling is set about 5cm/2in in from the edge and is pale golden on the surface (it will set completely as it cools). Leave to cool in the pan for 10 minutes, then transfer the tart to a flat serving plate. Sprinkle with nutmeg and a light dusting of icing sugar. Serve warm or cold.

Bitter chocolate tart with coffee bean syrup

With its ultra-sophisticated sauce of dark-roast coffee beans, Phil Vickery has created the perfect dinner party dessert.

Serves 6-8

250g/9oz shortcrust pastry
clotted cream, to serve

for the coffee bean syrup
250g/9oz sugar
25g/1oz dark-roast coffee beans

for the filling
250g/9oz good-quality plain
    chocolate
150g/5½oz white chocolate, broken
    into pieces
100 g/3½oz unsalted butter
100 g/3½oz caster sugar
3 eggs, plus 4 extra yolks

1 Preheat the oven to 200°C / 400°F / gas 6. Roll the pastry out and use to line a 23cm/9in round loose-bottomed flan tin. Lightly prick the pastry with a fork, then line with greaseproof paper and fill with baking beans. Bake for 15 minutes. Remove the beans and paper, then bake for 8-10 minutes more, until the pastry is pale golden. Set aside to cool.

2 Make the syrup: in a small pan, warm 250ml/ 9fl oz water with the sugar over a low heat, stirring occasionally, until the sugar has dissolved. Add the coffee beans and bring to the boil. Reduce the heat and simmer for 4 minutes. Remove from the heat and discard all but 12 of the coffee beans. Leave these in the syrup and set aside to cool.

3 Make the filling: break 150g/5½oz of the plain chocolate into small pieces and place in a heatproof bowl with the white chocolate and the butter. Set the bowl over a pan of simmering water and stir occasionally until all the chocolate has melted. Remove the bowl from the heat and set it aside.

4 In a clean bowl, whisk together the caster sugar, eggs and extra yolks for about 10 minutes, until thickened. Grate the remaining plain chocolate and sprinkle it over the pastry case, then pour over the filling. Bake for 8 minutes, until lightly set, remove and leave to cool, then chill.

5 Serve the tart cut into wedges with a little coffee bean syrup and some clotted cream.

The Bitter chocolate tart with coffee bean syrup, opposite, served with a gobbet of clotted cream, makes the most sophisticated and alluring of plates.

Pear crumble tart

Serves 6

100g/3½oz plain flour
100g/3½oz self-raising wholemeal
    flour
1tsp ground mixed spice
100g/3½oz butter, cut into small
    pieces
50g/2oz light muscovado sugar
2 large ripe pears, such as Comice
100ml/3½fl oz crème fraîche
1 egg, lightly beaten
2tsp caster sugar

1 Sift the flours and spice together in a bowl. Add the butter and rub it in with your fingertips until the mixture has the consistency of fine breadcrumbs. Transfer about a quarter of the mixture to a separate bowl and stir the muscovado sugar into this to make the topping.

2 Preheat the oven to 190°C / 375°F / gas 5. Add about 2 tablespoons of cold water to the unsweetened crumble and mix to a firm dough. Knead briefly on a lightly floured surface, then roll out and use to line a 20cm / 8in deep flat flan tin or pie plate. Chill for 20 minutes.

3 Line the crumble case with greaseproof paper and baking beans. Bake blind for 20 minutes, then reduce the oven setting to 180°C / 350°F / gas 4.

4 Peel and core the pears, then cut the flesh into small pieces; spread evenly over the flan case. Mix the crème fraîche, egg and caster sugar, then spread over the pears. Sprinkle with the reserved crumble topping and bake for 45-50 minutes until the topping is crisp and golden.

5 Serve warm or cold.

Lemon and almond tart

Lemon tarts have enjoyed a considerable vogue over the last couple of years. This version is less aggressively lemony than some and has a delicious texture from the ground almonds.

Serves 6

225g/8oz sweet or plain
   shortcrust pastry
2 eggs
150g/5oz icing sugar
4 lemons
100g/3½oz butter, melted
75g/2½oz ground almonds
icing sugar, to dust

1 Preheat the oven to 220°C/425°F/gas 7. Roll out the pastry on a lightly floured surface and use to line a 20cm/8in tart pan. Bake blind for 10 minutes, remove the greaseproof paper and beans and return the pastry case to the oven for a further 8-10 minutes until the pastry is crisp and golden, then reduce the oven setting to 180°C/350°F/gas 4.
2 In a bowl, whisk the eggs and icing sugar together until fluffy. Mix in the grated zest of 2 of the lemons, the butter, ground almonds and juice of all 4 lemons. Don't worry if the mixture looks curdled — it won't affect the final result.
3 Pour the filling into the pastry case and bake for 25 minutes until the filling is set. Leave to cool and serve dusted with icing sugar.

Pear and kumquat tart

Serves 8

for the shortbread
225g/8oz plain flour
150g/5oz butter, cubed
50g/2oz caster sugar
1 egg yolk

for the filling
2 pears
100g/3½oz unsalted butter,
   softened
100g/3½oz caster sugar
2 eggs, beaten
100g/3½oz ground almonds
15g/½oz plain flour
8 kumquats
225g/8oz apricot jam or apple jelly
1tsp fresh lemon juice
thick Greek-style yoghurt, to serve

1 Lightly grease a 25cm/10in flan pan.
Make the shortbread: place the flour in a
bowl and rub in the butter with your fingertips
until the mixture has the consistency of fine
breadcrumbs. Stir in the sugar, then make a
well in the centre and mix in the egg yolk to
bind. Gather up the shortbread mixture in
your hand and press into a ball, wiping the
bowl clean.
2 Roll out the shortbread mixture between
2 sheets of waxed paper. Remove the waxed
paper and line the flan pan with the
shortbread, using your fingers to press it in
and fill any gaps. Cover the shortbread with
plastic film and chill for 30 minutes while you
make the filling.
3 Preheat the oven to 200°C/400°F/gas 6.
Make the filling: core and quarter the pears
and leave in a bowl of water. Meanwhile,
cream the butter and sugar with an
electric hand-beater until light and fluffy.
Beat in the eggs, followed by the almonds
and flour. Spoon into the chilled base and
spread evenly.
4 Drain and dry the pears. Make several thin
parallel cuts across each quarter, taking care

not to cut right through. Lift each quarter
with a palette knife and arrange on the filling
like the spokes of a wheel. Cut one of the
kumquats in half and slice the rest. Place half
a kumquat in the centre of the tart and cut
the other into slices and arrange all the slices
around the pears.
5 Bake for 10 minutes, then reduce the oven

setting to 180°C/350°F/gas 4 and bake for
20-25 minutes until golden brown.
6 Make the glaze: in a small pan, gently heat
the jam and lemon juice for 1-2 minutes.
Pass this glaze through a fine sieve into a
bowl, then remove the tart from the oven and
brush the glaze over it. Serve warm or at
room temperature, with Greek-style yoghurt.

Caramelized banana tarts with vanilla custard

Bananas and custard are a marriage made in heaven. A cinnamon sugar glaze takes this pud out of the nursery.

Makes 4

75g/2¾oz plain flour
2tsp icing sugar
45g/1½oz margarine or butter
1 medium egg yolk, lightly beaten
2tbsp caster sugar
½tsp ground cinnamon
1 recipe quantity of custard (see page 40)
2 bananas, thinly sliced
juice of 1 lemon
a few drops of vanilla extract

1 Preheat the oven to 190°C/375°F/gas 5. Sift the flour and icing sugar together and rub in the margarine or butter until the mixture has the consistency of breadcrumbs. Mix with the egg yolk and enough water to bind it without making it sticky. Divide the dough into 4 pieces. Roll out each quarter to a thin circle, 12.5cm/5in in diameter. Use to line 4 shallow Yorkshire pudding moulds, 10cm/4in in diameter. Prick with a fork and chill for 20 minutes.

2 Bake the flan cases for about 20 minutes until crisp and pale golden. Meanwhile, mix together the sugar and cinnamon.

3 Make the custard as described on page 40. Keep it warm.

4 Preheat the grill to high. Put the flan cases on the grill rack. Toss the bananas in the lemon juice. Arrange the banana slices in the pastry cases to cover. Sprinkle the cinnamon sugar thickly over the fruit and grill for 2-3 minutes until the tops are bubbling and golden.

5 Arrange the tarts on individual plates, stir the vanilla extract into the custard and spoon this around them. Serve immediately.

Mixed berry pie

Serves 4

85g/3oz porridge oats
150g/5oz desiccated coconut
125g/4½oz butter, softened

for the filling

3tbsp plain flour
pinch of salt
50g/2oz caster sugar
3 egg yolks
300ml/½ pint milk
grated zest of 1 lemon
3tbsp thick double cream
350g/12oz mixed soft berries
   (strawberries, raspberries,
   redcurrants and blackberries)

1 Preheat the oven to 150°C/300°F/gas 2. Mix together the oats, coconut and butter and press firmly into the base and sides of a 20cm/8in loose-bottomed flan pan. Bake for 15 minutes, then allow to cool.
2 Make the filling: sift the flour and salt into a bowl. In another large bowl, beat the sugar and egg yolks together until thick and creamy, then gradually mix in the flour.
3 Heat the milk and lemon zest in a small pan. Bring to simmering point, allow to cool slightly and then pour into the flour mixture, stirring constantly. Tip into a small pan and bring to the boil. Cook, stirring constantly until thickened; about 2 minutes.
4 Allow to cool, stirring occasionally to prevent a skin forming. Fold in the cream and pour into the pie case. Pile the berries on top. Chill and serve with cream.

Satsuma and raisin tart

Serves 4-6

225g/8oz shortcrust pastry, thawed if
   frozen
175g/6oz seedless raisins
2tbsp light muscovado sugar
4 satsumas
2 bananas, mashed
50g/2oz ground almonds
beaten egg or milk, to glaze
175g/6oz thick Greek-style yoghurt,
   to serve

1 Preheat the oven to 200°C/400°F/gas 6. Set aside a quarter of the pastry and roll out the rest on a floured board into a round a little larger than a 20cm/8in pie dish. Use to line the pie dish and trim the edges.
2 Mix together the raisins and sugar. Peel and segment the satsumas over the raisin mixture to catch any juices, then cut the segments into pieces. Stir the satsuma pieces into the raisin mixture, together with the bananas and almonds, then spoon into the pastry case; level the surface.
3 Roll out the reserved dough into a 23cm/9in long strip and cut it lengthwise into narrow strips. Arrange the strips over the filling to form a lattice pattern, sticking down the ends with a little water. Brush with beaten egg or milk to glaze.
4 Bake for about 25 minutes until just set. Serve either warm or cold, cut into wedges and topped with a generous dollop of Greek-style yoghurt.

French apple tart

This wonderfully rich, tangy fruit tart comes from the Alsace region of France. The flavour of the apples is all-important and many of the fragrant English varieties work very well. Depending on the time of year, try crisp juicy Jonagold or catch the end of the sharply sweet Cox's season or choose one of the lesser known types now making their appearance in the shops. All of these varieties hold their shape, which makes them perfect for slicing.

Serves 6-8

for the pastry
175g/6oz plain flour
pinch of salt
85g/3oz butter, chilled and cut into small pieces
25g/1oz caster sugar
1 egg yolk

for the filling
9 crisp eating apples
juice of 1 lemon
50g/2oz caster sugar
knob of butter
175g/6oz apricot jam

1 Sift the flour and salt into a bowl or food processor. If making the pastry by hand, rub the butter into the flour until it has the consistency of fine breadcrumbs. Stir in the sugar, egg yolk and 2 tablespoons of water, then work to a dough. If using a processor, add the butter and sugar to the flour and salt; whiz for 10-15 seconds. Add the egg yolk and 2 tablespoons of water and process until the mixture forms a dough. Wrap in plastic film and chill for 30 minutes.
2 Preheat the oven to 200°C / 400°F / gas 6. Prepare filling: peel, core and chop 6 of the apples; place in a pan. Add half the lemon juice and 2 tablespoons of water. Cover and cook over a low heat for 15-20 minutes, stirring occasionally, until tender. Stir in half the sugar and all the butter; cook for 2-3 minutes, stirring to a pulp.
3 Meanwhile, roll out the chilled dough and use to line a 25cm / 10in loose-bottomed flan pan. Prick the base all over with a fork. Line the pastry case with greaseproof paper, fill with a layer of beans

and bake blind for 10 minutes. Remove the paper and beans and return to the oven for 5 minutes.
4 Reduce the oven setting to 180°C / 350°F / gas 4. Peel, quarter, core and thinly slice the last 3 apples; toss the slices in the remaining lemon juice and sugar. Spread the apple purée over the pastry and arrange the apple slices on top (save the smaller apple slices for the inside circular layer of the tart as they tend to be easier to arrange). Bake for 30 minutes until golden.
5 Leave the tart to cool slightly, then carefully remove from the pan. Meanwhile, gently heat the jam and 1 tablespoon of water in a pan and boil for 1-2 minutes until thickened. Push the jam through a sieve into a bowl and brush this glaze evenly over the tart. Serve warm or cold.

Notes:
* A food processor makes light work of pastry, but take care not to over-process or the pastry texture may be tough.

Oranges and lemons basket

Serves 4-6

for the pastry
175g/6oz plain flour
75g/2¾oz butter, cut into small pieces
25g/1oz caster sugar

for the filling
3 oranges
2 lemons
300ml/½ pint single cream
85g/3oz caster sugar
2 eggs, beaten

1 Make pastry: place flour in a bowl, add butter and rub in until consistency of fine breadcrumbs. Stir in sugar, add 2 tablespoons water and mix to a firm dough. Wrap in film and chill 30 minutes.
2 Preheat the oven to 200°C / 400°F / gas 6. Knead the pastry and roll out on a floured board, then use to line a 17.5cm / 7in flan pan. Trim the edge off and twist a wide strip of foil around the edge of the flan pan to hold the decoration.
3 Roll out the trimmings and cut into long thin strips. Brush edge of tart with water. Twist two long strips of pastry together and press around the edge. Twist two shorter lengths of pastry together and place on one side to form a handle. Make two more handles and attach to the sides.

4 Line pastry case with greaseproof paper and fill with beans. Bake for 15 minutes, then remove beans and paper and return to oven for 5 minutes. Reduce the oven setting to 180°C / 350°F / gas 4.
5 Make filling: grate zest from 1 orange and 1 lemon. Place in bowl with cream, 50g / 2oz of sugar and the eggs. Beat together, then pour into flan case. Bake for 25-30 minutes or until just set.
6 Squeeze juice from 1 orange into small pan with rest of sugar and a few thinly sliced strips orange and lemon peel. Heat gently to dissolve sugar, then boil for 2 minutes until slightly syrupy.
7 Remove the rind and pith from remaining oranges and lemons and slice thinly. Arrange over tart and pour over the syrup and peel. Serve cold.

Blueberry and cranberry tartlets

Serves 6

225g/8oz sweet shortcrust pastry,
    thawed if frozen
flour, for rolling

for the filling

250g/9oz ricotta cheese
50g/2oz caster sugar
1tsp vanilla extract
150ml/¼ pint double cream
1tbsp plain flour, sifted
200g/7oz fresh or frozen cranberries
    and blueberries

for the topping

3 medium egg yolks
40g/1½ oz caster sugar
3tbsp kirsch (cherry brandy)

1 Preheat the oven to 190°C / 375°F / gas 5. On a lightly floured surface, roll out the pastry and use to line six 9cm / 3¾in fluted tartlet pans. Prick the bases with a fork and line with greaseproof paper and baking beans. Bake for 10 minutes, remove the paper and beans and set aside to cool.
2 Thoroughly beat together all the filling ingredients, except the blueberries and cranberries, until smooth. Divide the mixture between pastry cases and top each tartlet with the blueberries and cranberries.
3 Place all the topping ingredients in a bowl and place over a pan of simmering water. Whisk with an electric hand-whisk until the mixture becomes thickened and creamy. Spoon a little of the mixture over each of the tartlets. Place on a baking sheet and bake for 15-20 minutes until

golden and lightly set. Allow to cool for 5 minutes then remove from the tartlet pans and serve.

Variation:
Try making this with any mixture of berry fruit and flavouring it with any fruit liqueur.

Cranberry and almond tart

This is a delicious tart to make from the Christmas baking leftovers.

Serves 6

225g/8oz shortcrust pastry, thawed if
   frozen
100g/3½oz butter, softened
100g/3½oz caster sugar
2 medium eggs
½tsp orange flower water (optional)
25g/1oz plain flour
100g/3½oz ground almonds
25g/1oz fresh breadcrumbs
350g/12oz frozen cranberries,
   defrosted slowly in the fridge
2tbsp apricot jam or redcurrant jelly
2tbsp whole blanched almonds,
   toasted and roughly chopped

1 Preheat the oven to 190°C / 375°F / gas 5. Roll out the pastry and use it to line a 20cm / 8in flan pan. Line with foil and dried beans and chill for 30 minutes. Bake the pastry case blind for 15 minutes, then remove the foil and beans and set aside.
2 Beat together the butter and sugar until pale and fluffy, then gradually add the eggs and the orange flower water, if using it. Gently fold in the flour, followed by the ground almonds.
3 Scatter the breadcrumbs over the pastry case to soak up the fruit juices and prevent the pastry becoming soggy. Spoon about three-quarters of the cranberries into the case in a single layer. Spoon, then spread, the almond mixture over.
4 Bake in the centre of the oven for 30 minutes, until the mixture springs back when lightly pressed.
5 In a small pan, gently heat the apricot jam or redcurrant jelly with 1 tablespoon of water until melted. Add the remaining cranberries and warm through gently until the berries burst. Spoon on to the tart and then scatter the almonds over.

Variations
* Replace the cranberries with frozen redcurrants, blackcurrants, or raspberries.
* Use half a jar of high-fruit, jam or conserve in place of the fruit, omitting the breadcrumbs.
* Scatter untoasted almonds over the sponge before baking.
* Sift icing sugar over to serve.

Soured cream apple crumb pie

Serves 8

for the pastry
250g/10oz plain flour
pinch of salt
75g/3oz butter
50g/2oz vegetable fat
4-5tbsp cold water
for the filling
1 lemon
1tbsp plain flour
1tbsp caster sugar
142ml/¼pint carton of soured cream
4 eating apples, such as Braeburn

for the topping
50g/2oz light muscovado sugar
75g/3oz plain flour
½tsp ground cinnamon
50g plus 1tbsp/2oz butter at room
   temperature, cut into pieces

1 Make pastry as for American pie crust pastry (see page 84). Roll out on a lightly floured surface to fit a round 23x5cm / 9x2in deep pie dish or pan. Trim edges, then roll out trimmings and cut out leaf shapes and make berries. Arrange around top edge of pie, overlapping slightly and securing with a little water. Chill for 15 minutes.

2 Preheat the oven to 230°C / 450°F / gas 8. Make the filling: grate the zest from the lemon and squeeze 2 teaspoons of juice. In a large bowl, mix the lemon juice and zest, flour, sugar and soured cream. Peel and core the apples, and cut them into wedges. Stir the apple wedges into the bowl and spoon into the pastry case.
3 Make the topping: mix all the ingredients with your fingers until you have coarse crumbs. Press the mixture lightly together to form loose clumps, then scatter over the pie. Bake for 10 minutes, then lower the setting to 180°C / 350°F / gas 4 and bake for 30-35 minutes until the apples are tender. Serve warm.

Puff the magic pastry

Dovedale, pear and pecan puffs

Roll out 450g / 1lb puff pastry to 5mm / $\frac{1}{4}$in thick.
Cut out four 12.5cm / 5in circles and knock up
sides with back of a knife. Chill. Beat 1 egg yolk
with a teaspoon of water, then brush over circles,
taking care not to let it dribble over sides as this
stops rising. With side of a fork, score lines 2cm /
$\frac{3}{4}$in long around edges and prick inner area. Chill.
Preheat oven to 220ºC / 425ºF / gas 7. Whisk egg
white to soft peaks, then gently mix in 100g /
$3\frac{1}{2}$oz crumbled Dovedale (or other blue) cheese.
Fold in $2\frac{1}{2}$ tablespoons chopped pecans with 2
teaspoons cream, and pinch each thyme and
pepper. Chill. Peel and core 4 pears, reserving
stalks. Cut each into 16 slices. Melt 25g / 1oz
butter with $\frac{1}{4}$ teaspoon sugar in a large frying
pan, then cook half the slices until softened and
lightly brown. Cook rest in same way, then cool.
In centre of each pastry circle, pile a quarter of
filling and arrange pear slices around it. Bake for
15 minutes until golden. Stick pear stalk in centre
and scatter with a little more thyme and pecans.

Tropical mango tart

Preheat oven to 200ºC / 400ºF / gas 6. Roll out
250g / 9oz puff pastry and cut out 30x20cm /
12inx8in rectangle. Place on greased baking sheet
and prick with a fork. Spread 2 tablespoons of
lemon curd over the pastry, leaving a 2.5cm / 1in
border. Arrange drained mango slices from two
400g / 14oz cans (in syrup) in overlapping rows to
cover lemon curd, leaving a 1cm / $\frac{1}{2}$in border of
pastry. Using back of a knife, make a small rim
around the pastry edges, then bake for about 20-
25 minutes until the pastry is golden brown and
cooked through. Decorate the tart with coconut
shavings and serve hot or cold.

Quick rhubarb tarts

Serves 2

Preheat the oven to 200ºC / 400ºF / gas 6. Roll out 175g / 6oz puff pastry and cut out 2 circles, each measuring about 12.5cm / 5in in diameter. Transfer to a greased baking sheet and prick all over with a fork. Cook for 8 minutes until puffed and lightly golden. Meanwhile, put 175g / 6oz chopped rhubarb, 1 tablespoon caster sugar and 1 teaspoon ground ginger in a small pan with 2 tablespoons water. Simmer for 4 minutes, until the rhubarb is tender. Stir in 1 tablespoon ground almonds and spoon mixture on top of the pastry rounds. Sprinkle over 2 teaspoons demerara sugar and cook for a further 5 minutes, until golden. Serve hot with crème fraîche or custard.

Pear and walnut slices

Serves 4

Preheat the oven to 200ºC/400ºF/gas 6. Roll 150g/5½oz puff pastry out to a thickness of about 3mm/⅛in and cut it into four 9x11cm/3½x4½in rectangles. Place on a large baking sheet. Use a knife to score a 1cm/½in border around the edges and mark with a criss-cross pattern. Peel, halve and core 2 firm but ripe pears. Then thinly slice the pears, not cutting all the way through at the top of each pear. Lift a halved pear on to each pastry rectangle and fan out the slices. Brush the pears with lemon juice and sprinkle with 2 table-spoons sugar. Bake for 20 minutes until the pastry is golden and well risen. Remove from the oven, brush with 2 tablespoons maple syrup and scatter 25g/1oz walnut pieces over it. Serve warm with cream.

Tarte tatin

Serves 6

350g/12oz puff pastry
6-8 firm, crisp eating apples, such
  as Cox's
150g/5½ oz unsalted butter, at
  room temperature
175-215g/6-7½ oz caster sugar,
  depending on the acidity of the
  apples
crème fraîche, to serve

1 Preheat the oven to 220°C / 425°F / gas 7. Roll out the pastry to a circle 30cm / 12in in diameter and 3-4mm / ⅛in thick — if it is any thicker than this it won't cook properly. Place on a board, cover and chill the pastry for at least 30 minutes.
2 Meanwhile, peel, core and halve the apples. Take a medium heavy-based, ovenproof frying pan (about 25cm / 10in) and, using a spatula, spread two-thirds of the butter evenly all over the base of the pan. Sprinkle over two-thirds of the sugar, again distributing it evenly over the base. Starting at the outside edge of the pan, arrange the apple halves, cut sides up, around the pan. After a full circle of halves is in place, fill the middle. Pack the apples closely together as they will shrink during cooking. Sprinkle the apples with the remaining sugar and dot with flakes of the remaining butter.
3 Place the pan over a medium-to-high heat and move it around slowly and carefully to distribute the heat evenly. Take care that the mixture does-

n't splash and that no part of the butter and sugar begins to burn or blacken. Cook until it has all turned golden and caramelized. This should take about 20-30 minutes.
4 Allow to cool a little, until steam stops rising. Carefully lay the chilled pastry circle on top of the apples. Tuck the edges down the sides of the pan so that, when it is inverted, the edges will hold in the apple, juices and caramel. Place the pan in the oven for 10 minutes until the pastry is puffed and golden. Reduce the oven temperature to 180°C / 350°F / gas 4 and cook for another 10–15 minutes, both the pastry is crisp.
5 Remove from the oven, leave to cool for about 5 minutes, then carefully loosen round the edges of the tart with a knife. Place a plate that is larger than the pan on top and quickly turn both upside down so that the tart inverts on to the plate. Using a palette knife, guide any apples which have become loose back into place; leave to cool.
6 Cut into wedges and serve with crème fraîche.

Quick apricot and pine nut tatin

Using tinned apricots allows you to make a stunning and delicious tarte tatin from store-cupboard ingredients.

Serves 6

400g/14oz frozen puff pastry,
  defrosted
50g/2oz butter
50g/2oz soft brown sugar
900g/2lb tinned apricot halves in
  syrup, drained
2tbsp Benedictine or Cointreau,
  (optional)
50g/2oz pine nuts
cream or ice cream, to serve

1 Preheat the oven to 200°C / 400°F / gas 6. Roll out the pastry to a circle 30cm / 12in in diameter and 3-4mm / ⅛in thick. Cover and chill the pastry for at least 30 minutes.
2 Take a medium heavy-based, ovenproof frying pan (about 25cm / 10in) and spread the butter evenly all over the base of the pan. Sprinkle the sugar over evenly. Starting at the outside edge of the pan, arrange the apricot halves, cut sides up, around the pan. After a full circle of halves is in place, fill the middle. Pack them closely together. Sprinkle over the liqueur if you are using one.
3 Place the pan over a medium-to-high heat and move it around slowly and carefully to distribute the heat evenly. Take care that no part of the butter and sugar burns or blackens. Cook until

uniformly golden and caramelized, 10-12 minutes.
4 Carefully lay the chilled pastry circle on top of the apricots. Tuck the edges down the sides of the pan so that, when it is inverted, the edges will create a rim that will hold in the fruit, juices and caramel. Place the pan in the oven for 12-15 minutes to cook the puff pastry.
5 Remove from the oven and carefully loosen round the edges of the tart with a knife. Place a plate or tray that is larger than the pan on top and quickly turn the pan upside down so that the tart inverts on to the plate. Leave to cool a little.
6 While the tart is cooling, toast the pine nuts carefully in a dry frying pan until nicely coloured.
7 Sprinkle the toasted nuts over the tart and serve, cut into wedges, with cream or ice cream.

Pear and almond tatin

Serves 6

for the pastry
200g/7oz plain flour
100g/3½oz butter, cubed
1 egg yolk
50g/2oz caster sugar

for the topping
50g/2oz butter
1.5kg/3lb pears, peeled, halved and
  cored
2tbsp brandy (optional)
2tbsp clear honey
2tbsp dark muscovado sugar
100g/3½oz marzipan, cubed
50g/2oz flaked almonds, toasted

1 Preheat the oven to 200°C / 400°F / gas 6.
To make the pastry, place the flour in a food
processor with the butter and blend until the
mixture has the consistency of fine breadcrumbs.
(Alternatively, mix the butter and flour in a bowl
and rub together with your fingertips to the
breadcrumb stage.) Add the egg yolk and sugar.
Mix to a firm dough. Chill for 30 minutes.
2 Heat the butter in a 23-25cm / 9-10in ovenproof
frying pan and arrange the pear halves, flat side
down, in a circle around the pan. Cook gently for
4-5 minutes, until they begin to soften, then turn
and cook the other side. Pour in the brandy, if
using it, and cook until the liquid has reduced.
Add the honey and sugar to the pan and cook for
4-5 minutes until the pears are caramelized and
a syrupy sauce has formed. Remove the pan from
heat.
3 Place a piece of marzipan between each pear.
Roll out the pastry and carefully lay on top of the
pears. Tuck the edges down the sides of the pan.
Bake for 20 minutes.
4 Invert on to a serving plate and scatter with the
toasted almonds to serve.

Treacle tart

Serves 10

for the pastry
225g/8oz plain flour
150g/5oz unsalted butter, diced
1 medium egg yolk
1tsp caster sugar
1-2tbsp cold water

for the filling
800g/1¾lb golden syrup
125g/4½oz white breadcrumbs
finely grated zest of 2 lemons
2 medium eggs, beaten
50g/2oz porridge oats
ice cream or whipped cream, to serve

1 To make the pastry, place the flour in a food processor with the butter and blend until the mixture has the consistency of fine breadcrumbs. (Alternatively, mix the butter and flour in a bowl and rub together with your fingertips to the breadcrumb stage.) Add the egg yolk, sugar and just enough cold water to mix to a firm dough. Place in a polythene bag and chill for 30 minutes.
2 Preheat the oven to 180°C / 350°F / gas 4. Roll out the pastry and use to line a shallow pie dish, about 25cm / 10in in diameter and 4cm / 1½in deep. Trim off the excess and flute the edges if desired.
3 To make the filling, warm the golden syrup in a pan until thinned but not hot. Remove from the heat and beat in the breadcrumbs, lemon zest, eggs and oats. Pour into the pastry case.
4 Bake for about 35 minutes, until the filling is just set and turning to golden. Allow to cool slightly and serve warm, with ice cream or whipped cream.

Deep South sweet potato pie with toffee pecans

Sweet potatoes can have pale or bright orange flesh. The taste is the same, but the orange looks prettier.

Serves 8

for American pie crust pastry
200g/8oz plain flour
pinch of salt
50g/2oz butter
50g/2oz vegetable fat
grated zest of 1 orange
icing sugar, for dusting

for the filling
550g/1lb 4oz sweet potatoes
1tsp grated orange zest
50g/2oz light muscovado sugar
2tsp mixed spice
2 eggs, beaten
450ml/¾pint single cream
3tbsp brandy

for the topping
25g/1oz butter
50g/2oz light muscovado sugar
5tbsp single cream
100g/3½oz pecan halves

1 Peel the sweet potatoes and cut them into chunks. In a pan of boiling water, cook them for about 10 minutes until tender. Drain well, then press through a sieve — you should have about 225g / 8oz. Set aside to cool.
2 Preheat the oven to 200°C / 400°F / gas 6. Make the American pie crust pastry: put the flour and salt in a large mixing bowl. Cut the butter and vegetable fat into pieces, then rub into the flour with your fingertips to make fine crumbs. Make a well in the centre, then, with a knife, stir in the orange zest and 3-4 tablespoons cold water — don't stir too much or the pastry will be tough — and lightly press together into a ball. You can do the rubbing and mixing in a food processor, adding only as much water as it takes to bind the mixture — then stop immediately.
3 Roll the pastry to fit a round 23x5cm / 9x2in deep pie dish or pan. Trim the edge with scissors to leave a 1cm / ½in overhang, then place a finger on the edge and push up the dough on either side with thumb and forefinger of your hand to make a wave. Line with greaseproof paper and baking beans or uncooked rice, and bake the pastry shell blind for 10 minutes.
4 Make the filling: mix together the sweet potato purée, the orange zest, sugar and mixed spice. Add the eggs and mix well. Gradually stir in the cream and brandy, then pour into the pie case. Bake for 40 minutes until the filling is just set. (It should be a bit wobbly in the centre.) Leave to cool slightly.
5 Make the topping: in a small pan, heat the butter and sugar, stirring, until the sugar has dissolved, then add the cream and simmer for 2-3 minutes until the mixture bubbles and is slightly thickened. Remove from the heat, add the pecans and toss, then spoon over the pie.
6 Dust the pie with icing sugar to serve.

Glossy choc and peanut butter pie

Serves 10

for the crust
200g/7oz digestive biscuits (about 14)
85g/3oz butter
2tbsp golden syrup

for the filling
225g/8oz full-fat soft cheese, at room
   temperature
150g/5½ oz chunky or coarse peanut
   butter
50g/2oz caster sugar
284ml/½ pint carton of whipping
   cream

for the topping
25g/1oz caster sugar
25g/1oz butter, in pieces
50g/2oz plain chocolate, broken into
   pieces
chocolate curls, to decorate

1 Preheat the oven to 180°C / 350°F / gas 4. Make the crust: seal the biscuits in a large polythene bag and crush well with a rolling pin. In a pan, melt the butter with the syrup, then stir in the biscuit crumbs until evenly coated. Press into the base and up the sides of a round 23x5cm / 9x2in deep pie dish or pan. Bake for 10 minutes, then leave to cool completely.
2 Make the filling: in a bowl, beat the soft cheese, peanut butter and sugar until well blended (an electric hand-beater makes this easier). Reserve 125ml / 4fl oz cream for the topping. Whip the remaining cream into very soft peaks, then fold into the peanut butter mixture. Spoon the mixture into the biscuit case.
3 Make the topping: in a pan, combine the sugar and reserved cream. Bring to the boil, stirring to dissolve sugar, then reduce the heat immediately and simmer, without stirring, for 5-6 minutes until very slightly thickened and pale yellow. Remove from the heat and stir in the butter and chocolate until melted; allow to cool slightly.
4 Pour the topping over the pie and spread to cover completely and evenly. Chill, uncovered, for about 1 hour until firm. Sprinkle with chocolate curls to decorate.

Note:
For a quick and easy way to make chocolate curls: run a vegetable peeler along the length of the flat side of a bar of chocolate at room temperature.

Amaretti and almond torte

Serves 6 (with second helpings)

300ml/½ pint double cream
3 large sprigs of rosemary
250g/9oz amaretti or macaroon
   biscuits
115g/4oz unsalted butter, melted
500g/1lb 2oz mascarpone
45g/1½oz caster sugar
finely grated zest of 1 lemon, plus
   1tbsp juice
1½tsp almond extract
200g/7oz Greek-style yoghurt
rosemary sprigs, roughly chopped
   toasted almonds, pistachio halves
   and icing sugar, to decorate
Amaretto liqueur, to serve

1 In a small pan, bring the cream and rosemary sprigs to the boil, then remove from the heat and leave to cool.
2 In a food processor or blender, grind the biscuits to fine crumbs, or put them in a freezer bag, seal and crush with a rolling pin. Reserve 5 tablespoons of the crumbs. Mix the rest with the butter, then press the mixture into the base of a 23-24cm / 9-9½ springform or loose-bottomed round cake pan and chill.
3 In a bowl, beat the mascarpone with the sugar, lemon zest and juice, and the almond extract until smooth and creamy. Remove the rosemary from the cream and discard. Add the cream, yoghurt and reserved biscuit crumbs to the mascarpone mixture. Beat into soft peaks, then spoon into the pan and swirl evenly over the base with a spoon. Chill overnight until firm.

4 To serve, cut into slices and place one slice in the centre of each serving plate. Decorate with rosemary sprigs and a few almonds and pistachios, dust lightly with icing sugar and spoon over some Amaretto.

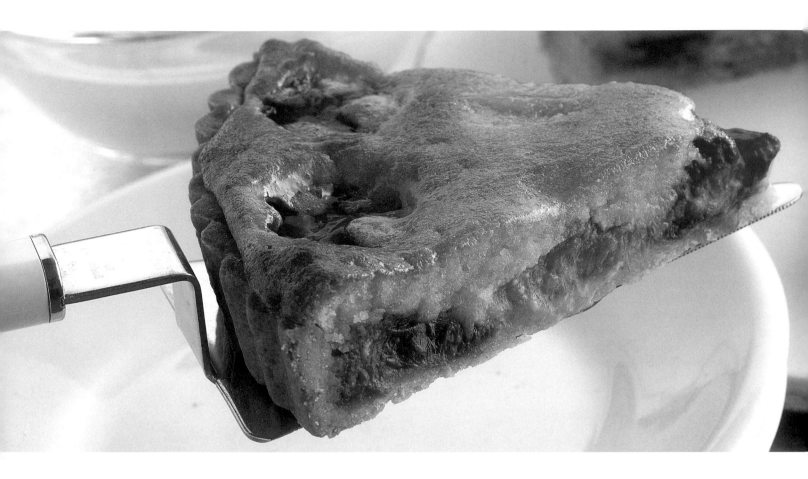

Plum, apricot and almond tart

Serves 16

for the pastry
350g/12oz plain flour
pinch of salt
200g/7oz unsalted butter, chilled
100g/3½oz icing sugar
2 medium egg yolks

for the filling
250g/9oz unsalted butter, softened
250g/9oz caster sugar
250g/9oz ground almonds
6 medium eggs
8 plums, halved and stoned
8 apricots, halved and stoned

for the glaze
1tbsp apricot jam, warmed

1 Preheat the oven to 200°C / 400°F / gas 6. Make the pastry: in a large bowl, sift the flour and salt together and rub in the butter until the mixture has the consistency of fine breadcrumbs. Stir in the icing sugar. Add the egg yolks and mix well to form a smooth ball. Wrap in plastic film and refrigerate for at least 20 minutes.

2 Lightly grease a 30cm / 12in loose-bottomed fluted tart pan and line the base with baking paper. Roll out the pastry and use to line the pan. Prick the pastry base, cover with greaseproof paper and baking beans and bake for 20 minutes until golden. Remove from the oven and reduce the setting to 180°C / 350°F / gas 4. Remove the paper and beans.

3 Meanwhile, prepare the filling: in a large bowl, cream together the butter and sugar until pale and fluffy. Add the ground almonds and mix well, then gradually beat in the eggs a little at a time. Arrange the plums and apricots, cut-side down, in the pastry case. Pour over the almond mixture, then bake for 35-40 minutes until set.

4 Brush the tart with the apricot jam, then serve with crème fraîche, if you like.

Smooth butterscotch tart

Serves 8

200g/7oz plain flour
100g/3½oz butter
small can of evaporated milk, chilled
175g/6oz light muscovado sugar
icing sugar and cocoa powder, for
    dusting
single cream, to serve

1 Preheat the oven to 200°C / 400°F / gas 6.
Tip the flour into a mixing bowl, add the
butter and chop it up into the flour with a
knife and fork. When the butter is in small
pieces, rub it into the flour with your
fingertips until the mixture looks like a pale
yellow crumble. Shake the bowl to make any
large lumps rise to the surface, then rub
these in too.
2 Using a round-bladed knife, mix 2-3
tablespoons of cold water into the crumble
until it starts to cling together. Pinch the
pastry together with your fingers, then wipe
the ball of dough around the bowl to pick up
stray crumbs.
3 On a lightly floured surface, knead the
dough gently until the pastry is as smooth as
you can get it. Roll it out into a 25cm / 10in
circle, then flip it over the rolling pin and
carefully roll it on a 20cm / 8in flan pan.
Press the pastry gently into the sides of the
pan, allowing the excess to flop over the
edge. Run the rolling pin over the top of the
pan to trim off the excess.
4 Line the pastry case with a circle of
greaseproof paper and fill with baking
beans, uncooked pasta or rice. Bake for 20
minutes, then remove the paper and beans.
5 In a bowl, using an electric hand-blender,
whisk together the evaporated milk and
sugar. After 5 minutes, the mixture should be
thickened and pale. Pour it into the pastry
case and return this to the oven for 10
minutes. (Surprisingly, the filling only takes
that time to set.) Allow the tart to cool in the
pan, then slide it out on to a serving plate.

6 Cut the tart into thin elegant slices and
dust them with icing sugar and cocoa powder.
Serve the slices of tart with a drizzle of
cream.

Note:
Make sure that you use authentic muscovado
sugar, and not soft brown sugar, or the filling
won't set properly.

Master class: making choux pastry

Paris-Brest

The Paris-Brest was created in 1891 by a baker whose shop was on the route of the annual bicycle race between Paris and Brest. The gâteau's origins explain not only its name but the circular shape, designed to mirror bicycle wheels.

Serves 6-8

for the choux pastry
150g/5oz plain flour
100g/3½oz butter
4 eggs, beaten
2tbsp flaked almonds
450ml/¾pint double cream
2tbsp icing sugar plus a little extra, to dredge
225g/8oz strawberries, halved
for the praline
85g/3oz unblanched almonds
85g/3oz caster sugar

1 Preheat the oven to 220ºC / 425ºF / gas 7. Make the choux pastry: lightly grease a large baking sheet, then line it with non-stick baking paper and draw a circle on it with a diameter of 18cm / 7in; set aside. Sift the flour on to a plate.
2 Gently heat the butter in a pan with 300ml / ½ pint water until melted, then bring to the boil. (To prevent excess evaporation, do not let the water boil until the butter has melted — then bring at once to a full rolling boil.) Remove from the heat, tip in the flour and beat thoroughly until the mixture is smooth and forms a ball, leaving the sides of the pan clean (1). (Do not over-beat — stop when the mixture is leaving the sides of the pan.) Allow to cool slightly.
3 Beat in eggs, a little at a time, until you have a smooth, shiny paste with a soft, dropping consistency. The mixture should fall reluctantly from a spoon if given a sharp jerk. Spoon 10 mounds of choux pastry around the circle on the baking paper (2), then sprinkle almonds on top. Bake for 40 minutes until

golden. Split the pastry ring in half and return to the oven for 5 minutes. Allow to cool on a rack. Choux pastry should be crisp on the outside and not doughy inside so it can encase a cream filling.
4 Make the praline: place the almonds, sugar and 1 tablespoon of water in a pan. Heat gently, stirring, until the sugar dissolves. Cook until the sugar caramelizes, turning occasionally. Pour on to an oiled baking sheet (3) and leave to harden for 15 minutes (4).
5 Grind the praline to a coarse powder using a

food processor or crush with a rolling pin. Whip the cream with 2 tablespoons of the icing sugar until it forms stiff peaks. Carefully fold the praline into the cream.
6 Spoon the cream mixture on to the bottom half of the pastry ring and push in most of the strawberries, reserving a few for decoration. Replace the lid and decorate with the reserved strawberries. Dredge the whole thing with icing sugar and serve immediately.

White chocolate choux puffs filled with lemon cream

Serves 8

for the pastry
150g/5oz plain flour
100g/3½ oz butter
4 eggs, beaten

for the filling
4 egg yolks
75g/3oz caster sugar
grated zest and juice of 2 lemons
50g/2oz butter, softened
300ml/½ pint double cream

for the decoration
50g/2oz white chocolate
icing sugar, for dusting

1 Preheat the oven to 200ºC / 400ºF / gas 6. Grease 2 baking sheets. Sift the flour on to a plate. Place the butter and 300ml / ½ pint water in a pan; bring slowly to the boil. When the liquid is boiling and the butter has melted, remove from the heat and tip in the flour all at once. Beat quickly until you have a soft ball that comes away from the sides of the pan.

2 Allow to cool for about 5 minutes, then gradually beat in the eggs to form a soft, shiny mixture. Dot heaped teaspoonfuls of the mixture over the baking sheets, allowing plenty of space for them to spread. Bake for 20-25 minutes until puffed and golden; remove from the oven and slit from one side three-quarters of the way through. Return to the oven for 5 minutes, then allow the choux puffs to cool on a wire rack.

3 Make the filling: place the egg yolks, sugar, lemon zest and juice in a small pan. Cook over a gentle heat for about 5 minutes, stirring, until the mixture has thickened. Don't allow to boil as the mixture will curdle. (If this does happen, sieve to remove lumps.) Remove from the heat and beat in the butter, then turn it into a bowl and cover tightly with plastic film. Allow to cool, then chill.

4 Up to 2 hours before serving, whip the cream until stiff, then fold it into the lemon sauce. Spoon a little lemon cream into each choux bun and set on a tray or cooling rack in one layer. Break the chocolate and melt in a bowl over a pan of hot, but not simmering, water. Drizzle the chocolate over the buns. When set, dust lightly with icing sugar and transfer to a serving plate.

Profiteroles with chocolate sauce

Serves 4-6

1 quantity of choux pastry (see previous pages)
300ml/½ pint double cream, whipped, plus 2tbsp
200g/7oz plain chocolate
25g/1oz butter
25g/1oz golden syrup

1 Make the pastry and cook the choux buns as described above. Using a piping bag, pipe whipped cream through the slit in the base of each bun. Pile on a serving plate.

2 Melt the chocolate, butter and syrup in a pan. Stir in the 2 tablespoons of cream and, just before serving, pour over the profiteroles.

Variations:
You can flavour the cream for filling the profiteroles with coffee or vanilla essence, or a liqueur, such as Tia Maria or Curaçao. Instead of the chocolate sauce, try simple caramel, or butterscotch sauce (page137), mocha sauce (page 12), chocolate fudge sauce (page 111), or even a thick raspberry coulis.

Note:
Choux pastry can be made in advance and kept in the fridge for a day before baking. When it is cooked, the buns can be stored in a tin for 2-3 days, or frozen: re-crisp in the oven.

Chocolate indulgence

Serves 6

65g/2½oz plain flour
50g/2oz unsalted butter
2 eggs, lightly beaten

for the chocolate paste
100g/3½oz plain chocolate, broken
   into pieces
2tbsp liquid glucose or golden syrup

for the coffee cream
450ml/¾pint double cream
5tbsp coffee liqueur
4tsp finely ground espresso or
   after-dinner coffee beans
175g/6oz plain chocolate
cocoa powder, for dusting

1 Preheat the oven to 220ºC / 425ºF / gas 7. Lightly grease and dampen 2 baking sheets. Sift the flour. Heat the butter in a pan with 150ml / ¼ pint water until the butter melts. Bring to the boil and add the flour all at once. Beat well with a wooden spoon until the mixture is smooth and leaves the side of the pan.
2 Allow to cool for 2 minutes, then gradually beat in the eggs to make a thick glossy paste. Place 18 teaspoons of the mixture, slightly apart, on the baking sheets.
3 Bake for about 20 minutes until well risen and golden. Make a slit in the side of each bun and bake for 2-3 minutes until crisp; allow to cool.
4 Make the chocolate paste: melt the chocolate and add the liquid glucose or syrup. Beat until the

mixture comes away from the sides of the bowl. Chill until firm, 30-60 minutes.
5 Make the coffee cream: lightly whip 150ml / ¼ pint of the cream with the coffee liqueur and spoon or pipe into the buns. Mix the coffee with 2 tablespoons hot water. Heat in a pan with the chocolate and remaining cream until the chocolate has melted; allow to cool.
6 Whip the chocolate cream until thickened. Use a little to secure three buns together on a plate. Spoon the remaining cream over the buns.
7 Cut the chocolate paste into 6. Roll out each piece as thinly as possible on a surface dusted with icing sugar. 'Polish' it by rubbing with the palm of your hand. Crumple to create folds and lay over the buns. Dust with cocoa powder.

Brandy snaps with chocolate cream

Makes about 25

85g/3oz unsalted butter
85g/3oz caster sugar
3tbsp golden syrup
85g/3oz plain flour
1tsp ground ginger
finely grated zest of 1 lemon
2tbsp brandy
100g/3½oz plain or white
   chocolate, broken into pieces
175g/6oz mascarpone cheese

1 Preheat the oven to 190°C / 375°F / gas 5. Line a baking sheet with baking paper. Melt the butter with the sugar and syrup. Remove from heat. Sift in the flour and ginger. Add the lemon zest and brandy; mix well.
2 Place 4 heaped teaspoons of mixture, spaced well apart, on the baking sheet. Bake for 8-10 minutes.
3 Leave on the baking sheet for about 30 seconds, then loosen one biscuit with a palette knife and roll around the handle of a large wooden spoon. Twist the spoon out. Repeat with the remaining biscuits; allow to cool. If they become brittle before shaping, return them to the oven for a few seconds.

4 Melt the chocolate, then lightly beat the cheese and mix with the chocolate until smooth. Fill the brandy snaps using a piping bag or small teaspoon.

Variation:
For dark and white chocolate fillings, use 50g / 2oz plain and 50g / 2oz white chocolate and beat each with half the mascarpone.

Millefeuille of raspberries and Florentine biscuits

Serves 2

35g/1¼oz unsalted butter
40g/1½oz caster sugar
15g/½oz plain flour
25g/1oz flaked almonds
60g/2¼oz mixed glacé fruits,
   such as cherries, melon,
   orange, pineapple and ginger,
   chopped
200ml/7fl oz whipping cream
1tsp orange-flavoured liqueur
25g/1oz raspberries, plus more to
   decorate
for the raspberry sauce
85g/3oz fresh raspberries
60g/2¼oz icing sugar, plus extra
   for dusting

1 Preheat the oven to 180°C / 350°F / gas 4. Line a baking sheet with non-stick baking paper. Lightly grease six 6x7cm / 2½inx2¾in metal cooking rings and place on a baking sheet.
2 Melt the butter in a pan with the caster sugar. Stir in the flour, almonds, chopped fruit and 2 tablespoons of the cream. Spoon the mixture into the cooking rings and bake for about 8 minutes, or until golden. Leave to cool, then remove from the rings and break up 2 of the biscuits.
3 In a bowl, whip the remaining cream to soft peaks; fold in the biscuits, liqueur and berries.
4 Make the raspberry sauce by blending the raspberries with the icing sugar in a food processor; sieve to make a smooth sauce.
4 Place a biscuit in the centre of each serving plate. Place a cookie ring on top as a guide, then fill with the raspberry cream. Carefully remove the rings and place a second biscuit on top of each. Spoon the sauce around. Lightly dust with icing sugar and decorate with raspberries.

Mincemeat, apple and marzipan strudel

Serves 6-8

350g/12oz good-quality mincemeat
2 eating apples, peeled, cored and
    grated
175g/6oz marzipan, chopped
6 sheets of filo pastry
25g/1oz butter, melted
icing sugar, for dusting

1 Preheat the oven to 200°C / 400°F / gas 6. Mix the mincemeat, grated apple and marzipan. Place 2 sheets of pastry, slightly overlapping, on a greased baking sheet. Brush with butter and place 2 more sheets on top, brush with butter and cover with remaining pastry.
2 Spread the mincemeat along one long pastry edge to within 2.5cm / 1in of the ends. Fold in the ends and roll up the pastry loosely. Brush with the remaining butter and mark several times with a sharp knife.

3 Bake for 30-35 minutes until the pastry is golden. Dust with icing sugar and serve warm.

Variation:

Macerate the mincemeat in a little brandy, Calvados or rum for an hour or two (or overnight) beforehand.

Apple and pecan filo pie

Serves 4-6

10 sheets of filo pastry
50g/2oz butter, melted
½ tsp ground cinnamon
6 eating apples, such as Cox's or
    Worcester
2tbsp lemon juice
50g/2oz caster sugar
50g/2oz pecan nuts
50g/2oz raisins or sultanas
4tbsp apricot jam
sieved icing sugar, for dusting

1 Preheat the oven to 190°C / 375°F / gas 5. Trim the filo pastry to make squares. Place 1 sheet of pastry in a greased 20cm / 8in flan pan. Mix the butter and cinnamon, then brush this over the pastry. Place a second sheet of pastry over the first one, but at a different angle. Continue layering the pastry, at slightly different angles and brushing between each layer, until the pastry is all used up.
2 Peel, core and slice the apples, then toss them in the lemon juice and sugar. Pile into the pastry case. Bake for 20-25 minutes until the pastry is golden and the apples are tender.

3 Sprinkle with pecan nuts and raisins or sultanas. Warm the jam and brush over the top. Dust with icing sugar and serve warm.

Variations:
Plump the dried fruit in brandy overnight for an extra kick to the flavour.
Grate some lemon zest and scatter a little over the butter between each layer of pastry.
You can use walnuts or hazelnuts in place of the pecans.

Filo apple strudels

Try to find shorter packets of filo pastry so you won't need to trim the pastry. Unused filo can be stored in the fridge for two days or in the freezer for one month.

Makes 8

8 sheets of filo pastry, about
    17.5x32.5cm/7x13in
100g/3½oz butter, melted
for the filling
350g/12oz cooking apples, peeled,
    cored and roughly chopped
juice of ½ lemon
85g/3oz demerara sugar
25g/1oz fresh brown breadcrumbs
50g/2oz sultanas
1tsp ground cinnamon
for the topping
2tbsp caster sugar
icing sugar, for dusting

1 Preheat the oven to 200°C / 400°F / gas 6 and lightly grease 2 baking sheets.
2 Prepare the filling: mix together the apple, lemon juice, sugar, breadcrumbs, sultanas and cinnamon in a bowl.
3 Unfold one sheet of filo pastry and brush liberally with melted butter. Spoon one-eighth of the apple mixture to cover the centre third of one long side of the pastry, leaving a small border, and bring the two short sides over the apple to cover it.
4 Roll the strudel over and over until the pastry is used up. Place on a baking sheet, then repeat the process with the remaining pastry sheets and apple mixture.

5 Brush the strudels with melted butter, then bake for about 15-20 minutes or until golden brown and crisp.
6 Meanwhile, make the topping: blend the caster sugar and 2 tablespoons of water in a small pan and heat gently until all of the sugar has dissolved. Spoon the syrup over the warm strudels and dust with icing sugar to serve.

Surrender to Chocolate

A soft-centred assortment of chocolate desserts

Chocolate brownie gâteau

The creamy chocolate filling here turns the humble brownie into something rather superior.

Serves 14-16

450g/1lb plain chocolate
225g/8oz unsalted butter, plus more
  for greasing
3 eggs
225g/8oz light muscovado sugar
75g/3oz self-raising flour
1tsp vanilla extract
175g/6oz pecan nuts, roughly
  chopped

for the filling
150ml/¼ pint double cream
100g/3½oz plain chocolate, broken
  into pieces

for the chocolate curls
100g/3½oz plain chocolate
100g/3½oz white chocolate

1 Preheat the oven to 190°C/375°F/gas 5. Grease 2 round 17.5cm/7in sandwich pans and line their bases with baking paper. Roughly chop 100g/4oz of the chocolate and set aside.
2 Break the remaining chocolate into pieces and melt, with the butter, in a bowl set over hot water. Beat together the eggs and sugar. Stir in the melted chocolate, sift in the flour and add the vanilla extract, the chopped nuts and chopped chocolate.
3 Divide between the sandwich pans and bake for about 30 minutes, until the surface has a sugary crust and feels firm. Loosen the edges with a knife and turn upside-down on a wire rack covered with greaseproof paper. Leave the cakes in the pans until cool, then remove the pans.
4 Make the filling: put the cream in a pan with the plain chocolate and heat gently until the chocolate melts. Allow to cool, then whisk until stiff and use to sandwich the cakes together.
5 Make the chocolate curls: melt the plain and white chocolate in separate bowls. Using a teaspoon, place thin lines of white chocolate on a marble slab or clean smooth baking sheet, leaving a gap of the same width between the lines. Fill the gaps with plain chocolate and leave to set. When just set but not brittle, push a sharp knife across the surface at an angle of about 45 degrees; alternatively, draw a potato peeler over the surface of the smooth side of a large chocolate bar to form curls, or use a clean, paper-stripping knife held at a slightly lower angle. Decorate the top of the cake with the curls.

(See picture on previous pages)

The chocolate brownies opposite can make the luscious dark heart of many desserts, topped with cloaking fruit and whipped cream, crème fraîche or ice cream.

Chocolate brownies

Makes 9

100g/3½oz plain chocolate, broken
  into pieces
175g/6oz butter, plus more for the
  pan
4 eggs
finely grated zest of 1 orange
150g/5oz light muscovado sugar
50g/2oz plain flour
50g/2oz ground almonds
50g/2oz plain chocolate chips
50g/2oz white chocolate chips
icing sugar and cocoa powder, to dust
ice cream, crème fraîche or whipped
  cream, to serve

1 Preheat the oven to 180°C/350°F/gas 4. Grease a 20cm/8in square cake pan and line it with baking paper. Melt the broken chocolate and butter together, stirring, and leave to cool once combined.
2 Whisk the eggs, orange zest and sugar together until frothy, about 3 minutes, then stir in the cooled chocolate and butter mixture. Fold in the flour and the ground almonds, followed by the plain and white chocolate chips.
3 Transfer to the prepared cake pan and bake for 30 minutes, until well risen and just firm to the touch. Leave the brownies to cool in the pan.
4 Cut into squares and dust with icing sugar and cocoa powder. Serve with ice cream, crème fraîche or whipped cream.

Variations:
For a classic American brownie, instead of the orange zest and juice, flavour the mixture with 1 teaspoon of good-quality vanilla extract.
You can also add 115g/4oz chopped pecans or walnuts with the chocolate chips; or try seedless raisins, chopped dates or figs, if you don't like nuts.

Master Class: making a roulade

Chocolate roulade

This is our version of the famous *bûche de Noël*, **the popular French Christmas gâteau. It looks rich but, as it isn't made with flour, it is light in texture and more like a mousse than a cake. Don't worry if it cracks while you are rolling it up – this is a typical feature of a good roulade.**

Serves 8-10

225g/8oz plain chocolate
4 eggs, separated
100g/3½oz caster sugar, plus a little extra
   for sprinkling
butter, for greasing
for the filling
300ml/½ pint double cream
225g/8oz canned natural chestnut purée
4tbsp icing sugar, plus a little extra for
   dusting
1-2tbsp brandy (optional)

1 Preheat the oven to 180°C/350°F/gas 4. Line a 23x33cm/9x13in Swiss roll tin with greased greaseproof paper. Break up 50g/2oz of the chocolate in a bowl and set over a pan of hot, not boiling, water. Stir until melted.
2 Pour the melted chocolate in a thin layer on a marble slab or cold upturned baking tray and leave to set. Holding a sharp knife at an angle of 45 degrees, shave off the surface of the chocolate to form curls. Place on greaseproof paper to set.
3 Melt the remaining chocolate as above. Whisk the egg yolks with the caster sugar for 5 minutes until pale and thick, then stir in the chocolate. Whisk the egg whites until stiff and fold into the mixture. Spread out in the prepared Swiss roll tin and bake for 15-20 minutes until risen and firm.
4 Sprinkle a piece of greaseproof paper with caster sugar. When the roulade is cooked, turn it out on to the paper and carefully peel off the lining paper. Cover the roulade with a warm, damp tea towel and leave to cool.
5 Make the filling: whip the cream until it

forms soft peaks. Reserve 5 tablespoons of it for decoration. Mix together the chestnut purée, icing sugar and brandy, if using it. Using a large metal spoon, fold the whipped cream into the chestnut purée mixture.

6 Spread mixture over roulade to within 1cm/½in of the edges. From one short end, roll it up, using the paper to help. Dust with sifted icing sugar. Swirl the reserved cream in the centre and scatter the chocolate curls on top.

Notes:
* When melting chocolate, fill the pan with hot, not boiling, water and remove from the heat before placing the bowl for melting the chocolate on top. Make sure that the bowl doesn't touch the hot water.
* You'll know when the chocolate has set properly because it won't stick to your hand when you touch it.
* Trim off any crisp edges from the roulade and you'll find that it is much easier to roll up.
* The roulade tends to shrink quite a bit, but that's quite normal.
* For best results, leave the roulade covered with the tea towel until completely cold, preferably overnight.
* To slice the roulade cleanly, first dip a long serrated knife into hot water. Wipe the blade with kitchen paper after cutting each slice and dip again in water.

Alternative chocolate roulade fillings:
* Purée 225g/8oz drained canned apricots by pushing them through a sieve and fold into 300ml/½ pint whipped double cream.
* Combine 300ml/½ pint whipped double cream with 225g/8oz frozen summer fruit. Serve when the fruit has completely defrosted, which takes about 2 hours.
* For a dark chocolate flavour, fold 50g/2oz melted plain chocolate and 2 teaspoons of coffee essence into 300ml/½ pint whipped double cream.

Torta al cioccolato (Chocolate tart)

The chocolate pastry for this tart doesn't need rolling – it is simply pressed into the tart pan.

Serves 12

for the pastry
100g/3½oz plain flour
25g/1oz cocoa powder
75g/2¾oz unsalted butter
25g/1oz ground almonds
50g/2oz caster sugar
1 egg, beaten
for the filling
50g/2oz butter
250g/9oz dark chocolate (look for
    one with 70% cocoa solids), broken
    into pieces
3 large eggs, separated
50g/2oz caster sugar
6tbsp double cream
1tbsp finely ground fresh coffee beans
icing sugar, for dusting
double cream or crème fraîche,
    to serve

1 Make the pastry: put the flour, cocoa powder, butter, ground almonds, sugar and egg in a food processor and whiz for about 10 seconds until the mixture forms a ball. Gather the dough together with your hands – the mixture should feel soft and slightly oily.
2 Press the dough into a flat even ball, then put this in the centre of a 2.5cm/1in deep 23cm/9in flan pan. Press the pastry evenly over the bottom of the pan with your fingers, then work it up the sides of with your thumbs. If the pastry feels thick around the sides, press with your thumbs to thin it out, letting the excess go over the edge (this can be trimmed off later). Cover with plastic film and chill for 30 minutes.
3 Preheat the oven to 200°C/400°F/gas 6. Level off the edges of the pastry case by running the rolling pin over the top. Prick the pastry base lightly with a fork, then line it with greaseproof paper and fill with baking beans or dried beans. Bake for 12-15 minutes, until the pastry no longer looks raw, then remove the paper and beans and

bake for 10-12 minutes more until the pastry feels firm. Leave to cool.
4 Make the filling: melt the butter and chocolate in a heatproof bowl set over a pan of gently simmering water; allow to cool slightly. Meanwhile, whisk the egg whites to very soft peaks. Don't worry if they separate a little as they stand. Whisk the yolks and sugar until just combined and slightly frothy, then stir in the cream and coffee. Pour the cooled chocolate into the coffee mixture and, using a large metal spoon, fold it in together with the egg whites. The mixture should be light and mousse-like in texture.
5 Spoon the mixture into the pastry case. For a smooth, shiny finish, heat a large palette knife under very hot running water. Shake off the water, then run the flat surface of the blade over the tart. Bake for 20 minutes. The tart should feel firm around the edges and be just set in the centre. Leave to cool.
6 Serve cold with a dusting of icing sugar and double cream or crème fraîche.

Mocha roulade

This feather-light chocolate roulade with a slight coffee crunch may be made the day before.

Serves 8

butter, for greasing
175g/6oz plain chocolate, in pieces
5 medium eggs, separated
175g/6oz caster sugar, plus more for
    dusting
85g/3oz chocolate coffee beans
300ml/½ pint double cream
icing sugar, for dusting
for the sauce
300ml/½ pint double cream
1tbsp finely grated strong-roast
    coffee, such as espresso
50g/2oz plain chocolate, in pieces
2-3 tbsp Kahlùa, Tia Maria or other
    coffee-flavoured liqueur

1 Preheat the oven to 180°C/350°F/gas 4. Grease a 35x25cm/14x10 inch Swiss roll tin and line with baking paper.
2 Melt the chocolate in a bowl set over a pan of gently simmering water or in a microwave cooker. Whisk the egg yolks and caster sugar until pale and lightly aerated. Using a balloon whisk, gradually blend in the melted chocolate.
3 Whisk the egg whites to soft peaks. Using a metal spoon, fold a quarter of the whites into the chocolate mixture to loosen it, then gently fold in the rest, taking care not to knock out too much air. Pour into the tin and spread into the corners.
4 Bake for 15-20 minutes, until risen and just firm.
5 Sprinkle caster sugar over a large sheet of greaseproof paper and invert the roulade on to it. Allow to cool.

6 Reserving a few chocolate coffee beans, coarsely chop the rest. Whip the cream until it just holds its shape, then stir in the chopped beans.
7 Peel the lining paper from the roulade and spread it with cream to within 1cm/½ in from the edge. Starting from a short end, roll it up and slide on to a plate, with the end join on the underside. Dust with icing sugar and keep in a cool place.
8 Make the sauce: gently heat half the cream and the coffee in a pan until almost boiling. Remove from the heat, then stir in the chocolate until melted. Stir in the remaining cream and the liqueur, then pour into a jug.
9 Serve the roulade with the sauce and decorated with the reserved beans.

White chocolate cheesecake

This cheesecake is dense and creamy, with the subtle taste of soft cheese and white chocolate. It is stunning served just as it is, but it is also wonderful decorated with strawberries and chocolate caraque.

Serves 8

for the base
200g/7oz plain chocolate digestive
   biscuits
50g/2oz unsalted butter
for the filling
300g/10½oz good-quality white
   chocolate, broken into pieces
400g/14oz full-fat soft cheese
150ml/¼ pint soured cream
2 eggs
1tsp vanilla extract
for the topping
8 fresh whole strawberries
dark chocolate curls, to decorate
   (page 102, optional)

1 Preheat the oven to 160°C/325°F/gas 3. Make the base: put the biscuits in a plastic bag and crush using a rolling pin. In a small non-stick pan, melt the butter then stir in the biscuit crumbs and mix well. Using the back of a metal spoon, press the mixture evenly into the bottom of a deep loose-bottomed 17.5cm/7in round cake pan; chill.
2 Make the filling: melt the chocolate (see previous pages). In a bowl, briefly stir the cheese, soured cream, eggs and vanilla extract together with a wooden spoon to blend lightly. Do not over-beat (too much air makes the cheesecake rise, then sink, or rise, then crack). Add the melted chocolate and stir until smooth (the mixture will thicken slightly).

3 Spread the mixture evenly over the biscuit base and level the top. Bake for 50 minutes until the mixture feels firm round the edge and is slightly soft but set in the middle (it is important not to overcook the cheesecake, or it will go grainy around the edge).
4 Remove from the oven and leave to cool. Carefully lift out of the cake pan and chill. When ready to serve, decorate with strawberries around the top and, if you are using them, arrange some chocolate curls in the centre.

Moist chocolate banana loaf

This is a speedy 'melt, mash and mix' recipe that cooks to a rich, sticky and delicious cake. Sliced thickly and served with ice cream, it makes an immensely satisfying easy dessert.

Makes a 900g/2lb loaf

150g/5oz butter, at room
   temperature, plus extra for greasing
150g/5oz light muscovado sugar
150g/5oz good-quality plain
   chocolate
2 medium bananas, mashed
3 eggs, beaten
200g/7oz plain flour
2tsp baking powder
strawberry ice cream, to serve
for the icing
100g/3½oz good-quality plain
   chocolate, broken into pieces
25g/1oz butter
50g/2oz icing sugar
1tbsp milk

1 Preheat the oven to 150°C/300°F/gas 2. Grease a 900g/2lb loaf pan and line it with greaseproof paper.
2 In a medium non-stick pan, gently heat the butter, sugar and chocolate until melted. Stir well and remove from the heat. Add the mashed banana and the eggs, then sift in the flour and baking powder. Mix to a smooth, thick batter.
3 Pour the mixture into the prepared loaf pan. Bake for 1 hour, until the cake has risen and feels firm in the centre when lightly pressed with your fingertips. Remove from the oven and allow to cool in the loaf pan for 5 minutes, then turn out on a wire rack to cool completely.

4 Make the icing: in a small non-stick pan, melt the chocolate with the butter. Sift in the icing sugar, then stir in the milk and beat well. Spread over the top of the cake only; using a flat-bladed knife, make swirls in the chocolate. Allow to set.
5 Serve cut into thick slices, with large scoops of strawberry ice cream.

Variations:
Add 25g/1oz chopped candied stem ginger to the mixture, or chopped ready-to-eat dried apricots, or some chopped pecans or walnuts.
Try flavouring the icing with a little orange-flavoured liqueur instead of the milk.

Dark chocolate puddings with white chocolate and Amaretto sauce

These can be made in next to no time, yet taste rich and special. They should have a moist, slightly gooey centre with a crisp crust, which contrasts beautifully with the custard-style white chocolate sauce.

Makes 4

100g/3½oz plain chocolate
100g/3½oz unsalted butter, plus
   extra for greasing
150g/5oz caster sugar
2 eggs, plus 2 extra yolks
55g/2oz plain flour

for the sauce

75g/2¾oz white chocolate
150ml/¼ pint double cream
1tbsp Amaretto or brandy
cocoa powder and mint sprigs, to
   decorate

1 Preheat the oven to 190°C/375°F/gas 5. In a pan set over a low heat, melt the plain chocolate and butter together until smooth; leave to cool slightly. Butter four 200ml/7fl oz ramekins.
2 In a bowl, lightly whisk together the sugar, eggs and extra yolks, then whisk in the melted chocolate. Sift in the flour and whisk together.
3 Pour the mixture into the ramekins and bake for 25 minutes until lightly risen and spongy to the touch. Turn off the heat but leave the puddings in the oven to keep warm.
4 Make the sauce: in a pan set over a low heat, melt the white chocolate with the cream until smooth. Remove from the heat and stir in the Amaretto or brandy.

5 Run a palette knife around each pudding and turn out, crust side up, on 4 shallow bowls and spoon a little sauce around each. Lightly dust the bowl and sauce with cocoa powder and decorate with a mint sprig.

Variations:

Add 50g/2oz plain or white (or a mixture) chocolate chips to the pudding mixture for a lovely contrast in texture.
If you haven't got time to make the sauce, simply serve the puddings with good-quality ice cream dressed with a dash of Amaretto or brandy.

White freezer cake with sticky brownie base

Keep one of these in the freezer at all times! The base is soft and sticky and the ice cream is simply the best.

Serves 12

for the brownie base
50g/2oz unsalted butter, plus extra
    for greasing
75g/2¾oz caster sugar
40g/1½oz dark muscovado sugar
50g/2oz good-quality plain
    chocolate
2tsp golden syrup
75g/2¾oz walnut pieces
1 egg
½tsp vanilla extract
25g/1oz flour
½tsp baking powder

for the ice cream
300g/10½oz good-quality white
    chocolate, broken into pieces
300ml/½ pint double cream
one 400g/14oz carton of ready-
    made vanilla custard

to decorate
50g/2oz plain chocolate
cocoa powder, for dusting

1 Preheat the oven to 180°C/350°F/gas 4. Lightly grease a 20cm/8in springform cake pan. In a small non-stick pan, gently heat the butter, sugars, chocolate and syrup, stirring until the mixture is smooth and the chocolate has melted. Stir in the walnuts, then remove from the heat and leave to cool.
2 In a bowl, beat together the egg and vanilla; add to the cooled mixture. Sift in the flour and baking powder, and mix well.
3 Pour into the prepared cake pan and bake for 15 minutes, until the outside is crisp and

beginning to shrink away from the sides but the centre is soft; leave to cool.
4 Make the ice cream: melt the white chocolate (see opposite). Whip the cream until just holding its shape, then whisk in the cold custard. Stir in the melted chocolate until the mixture is thick, smooth and well blended. Pour over the cooled brownie base and tilt the

cake pan to level the top.
5 Melt the plain chocolate for decoration. Using a teaspoon, drop 12 neat blobs on the ice cream, at regular intervals, 3cm/1¼in in from the edge. Draw a cocktail stick through the centre of each blob, in the same direction, to make hearts. Freeze for 4 hours until firm.
6 Serve dusted with cocoa powder.

Bitter chocolate puddings with chocolate fudge sauce

Phil Vickery's intensely flavoured little chocolate puddings please all palates.

Serves 8

225g/8oz butter, melted, plus extra
    for greasing
6 eggs
250g/9oz caster sugar
140g/5oz plain flour
50g/2oz cocoa powder
250g/9oz good-quality dark
    chocolate, cut into 5mm/¼in
    cubes
softly whipped double cream or
    ice cream, to serve

for the chocolate fudge sauce

300ml/½ pint double cream
175g/6oz unsalted butter
50g/2oz light muscovado sugar
175g/6oz good-quality dark
    chocolate, broken into pieces

1 Generously grease 8 individual (200ml / 7fl oz) pudding bowls or ramekins. In a large bowl, using an electric hand-blender, whisk the eggs with the sugar until really thick, about 10-15 minutes.
2 Sift the flour and cocoa together, then fold into the whisked mixture with a large metal spoon, making sure you don't knock out all the air. Fold in the melted butter and chocolate cubes, then spoon the mixture into the bowls or ramekins.
3 Cover the puddings tightly with foil, put them in a large pan and pour in enough boiling water to come halfway up the basins. Bring to a simmer and cover the pan. Steam for 45 minutes, until the puddings are firm to the touch.
4 Meanwhile, make the sauce: heat the cream, butter and sugar in a small pan, stirring, until the butter has melted. Add the chocolate and stir constantly until melted, then set aside (stir it occasionally to stop a skin forming).
5 When the puddings are ready, leave them to cool a little, then run a round-bladed knife around

the edge of each and invert on to a serving plate. Serve with scoops of cream or ice cream and drizzle over the sauce attractively.

Variation:

These little puddings also cook well in the microwave. Use microwave-proof bowls and cover them with microwaveable film. Microwave 2 or 3 three at a time on Medium for 3 minutes. Allow to stand for 1 minute before serving.
You can make one large pudding in a 1.75litre / 3 pint pudding basin. After filling, make a pleated tuck in the middle of a double thickness of grease-proof paper. Put it over the basin, tie firmly in place and trim off excess paper. Cover with a layer of pleated foil, tucking the edge under the greaseproof paper. Steam for 1¾ hours.

(See the picture opposite)

Zuccotto

Serves 12

100g/3½oz unblanched almonds
100g/3½oz blanched hazelnuts
150g/5oz plain chocolate
    (preferably with more than 55 per
    cent cocoa solids)
two 300g/10½oz slabs of Madeira
    cake
3tbsp cognac or brandy
5tbsp fresh orange juice
450ml/¾ pint double cream
100g/3½oz icing sugar
4tbsp apricot jam
icing sugar, for dusting

1 Toast the nuts in a dry frying pan. Roughly break up half the chocolate and melt in the microwave on High for 1 minute, or over a pan of simmering water (see page 102). Chop the remaining chocolate and reserve.
2 Line a 1.25litre / 2pint pudding basin with plastic film. Cut the cake into long vertical slices 1cm / ½ in wide (you are cutting down the length of the cake, not across as you would normally). Trim off the curved top from half of the slices, then cut these slices in half lengthwise on a slight diagonal to give you wedge-shaped pieces. Trim each slice to the depth of the inside of the basin, then arrange them, slightly overlapping, so they line the basin.
3 Cut a slice of cake to fit the bottom of the basin. Fill any gaps with small pieces of the cake. Mix the cognac or brandy and the orange juice. Spoon about two-thirds of this liquid over the cake in the

pudding basin, making sure it is evenly soaked.
4 Whip the cream until stiff. Fold in the nuts, icing sugar and chopped chocolate. Spoon half this mixture into the cake-lined basin; spread evenly over the base and sides, leaving a cavity in the centre.
5 Fold the melted chocolate into the remaining cream mixture. Spoon this into the cavity and smooth the top. Cover the top with the remaining cake, cutting the slices to fit. Spoon over the remaining orange juice mixture.
6 Cover with plastic film and chill overnight, or for up to 2 days.
7 To serve, remove the covering film and place a serving plate on top. Invert the basin on to the plate; carefully remove the bowl and peel off the plastic film. Warm the jam, then press through a sieve into a bowl. Brush the top and sides of the cake with jam glaze, then lightly dust with icing sugar. Serve cut into wedges.

Chocolate Magic

Cappuccino cups

Serves 4

Pour 150ml / ¼ pint whipping cream into a pan, sprinkle over 1 tablespoon powdered gelatine and leave to soften for 5 minutes. Heat gently until the cream just begins to simmer and the gelatine has melted, stirring constantly. Break 175g / 6oz plain chocolate into pieces, place in a food processor with cream mixture and whiz until chocolate has melted. Add handful of ice cubes, 300ml / ½ pint fromage frais, 50g / 2oz sugar and 1 tablespoon instant coffee powder. Whiz until smooth. Pour into cups and chill until set. Whip another 150ml / ¼ pint whipping cream and pare curls from a small chunk of plain chocolate with a vegetable peeler. Swirl the cream on the 'cups', dust with more coffee powder and decorate with the curls.

Magic chocolate pud

Serves 6

Preheat the oven to 180°C / 350°F / gas 4. Grease six 150ml / ¼ pint ramekins with butter. Cream together 50g / 2oz softened butter and 75g / 2³⁄₄oz dark muscovado sugar until lighter in colour and texture. Beat in 2 medium egg yolks. Sift together 40g / 1½oz self-raising flour and 2 tablespoons cocoa powder, and beat into the mixture. Gradually stir in 350ml / 12fl oz chocolate milk until smooth.

In a clean bowl, whisk the 2 egg whites and lightly fold into the chocolate mixture. Spoon into the prepared ramekins, place in a roasting pan and fill the pan with water, one-third of the way up the sides of the ramekins. Bake for 30 minutes or until the tops of the puddings spring back when lightly touched. The puddings separate to form a sponge on top and a layer of chocolate custard beneath. Serve hot, dusted with icing sugar.

Double-choc mud pie

Serves 6-8

Rub 90g / 3½oz lightly salted butter into 200g / 7oz flour with a pinch of salt until it resembles breadcrumbs. Mix in 1 egg yolk and enough cold water to give a soft dough. Wrap in foil and chill for half an hour. Roll out and use to line a 23cm / 9in round cake pan, then chill again. Preheat oven to 190ºC / 375ºF / gas 5. Melt 75g / 3oz plain chocolate with 4 tablespoons of cocoa powder and 25g / 1oz butter in a bowl over hot water. Allow to cool slightly. Cream 85g / 3oz butter with 225g / 8oz demerara sugar and slowly beat in 3 eggs. Stir in 150ml / ¼ pint single cream and the cooled chocolate mix, then pour into pastry case. Bake for 35-45 minutes until almost firm in the centre. Allow to cool. Whip 150ml / ¼ pint double cream to peaks, then spread it over the pie and grate 25g / 1oz plain chocolate over the top.

Banoffee pie

Ainsley Harriott's version of this modern classic.

Serves 6-8

Crush 100g / 3½oz each ginger and digestive biscuits in a plastic bag with a rolling pin as finely as possible. Mix 115g / 4oz butter with the biscuits and 1 teaspoon of mixed spice. Using a spoon, press into the base of 18-20cm / 7-8in flan pan lined with plastic film. Chill to set.

Put 115g / 4oz more butter in a pan, add a 400g / 14oz can of condensed milk and bring to boil, stirring all the time or it will burn. Reduce heat and simmer for 5-6 minutes, slowly stirring, until you have a light golden colour. Remove from the heat, beat in 2 tablespoons of double cream and cool.

Pour caramel on top of biscuit base. Slice 4-6 bananas and arrange half on top of caramel. Put another layer of banana on top. Sprinkle with cocoa powder, then chill. When ready to serve, whip 275ml / 10fl oz double cream, spoon on top, and dust with more cocoa powder to serve.

Hot Stuff

The warm embrace of baked and steamed puddings

Lemon and almond cake

Serves 8-10

175g/6oz soft butter, plus more for
   greasing
175g/6oz caster sugar
3 eggs
175g/6oz self-raising flour
50g/2oz ground almonds
grated zest and juice of 1 lemon
½tsp almond essence
to finish
2 lemons
2tbsp clear honey

1 Preheat the oven to 160ºC / 325ºF / gas 3.
Grease a 20cm / 8in loose-bottomed round cake
pan and line the base with baking paper.
2 Place the cake ingredients in a large bowl. Mix
well and beat with a wooden spoon or electric
whisk for 2-3 minutes, until light and fluffy.
3 Turn the mixture into the cake pan and smooth
the top. Pare the rind and pith from the lemons,
then slice the lemons into thin rounds. Arrange
these on top of cake.
4 Bake for 50-60 minutes until golden and firm.
Allow to cool in the cake pan for 5 minutes, then
release the sides and leave to cool further on a
wire rack.

5 Warm the honey and brush it over cake before
serving.

Variation:
Simply substitute orange zest and juice for the
lemon and oranges for the lemons on top to make
an orange and almond cake.

(See picture on previous pages)

Golden Apricot almond shortcake makes the sunniest of sweets, opposite.

Apricot almond shortcake

Serves 4

175g/6oz self-raising flour
50g/2oz caster sugar
75g/3oz butter or margarine, plus
   more for greasing
1 egg, plus 1 extra yolk
for the filling
50g/2oz ground almonds
50g/2oz plus 2tbsp caster sugar
grated zest and juice of 1 orange
white of 1 egg
400g/14oz can of apricot halves in
   their juice
icing sugar, for dusting

1 Preheat the oven to 190ºC / 375ºF / gas 5 and
grease a 20cm / 8in flan pan or pie plate. Put the
flour and sugar in a bowl and rub in the butter or
margarine until the mixture has the consistency
of fine breadcrumbs.
2 Make a well in the centre and mix in the whole
egg and the extra yolk to make a soft dough. Using
lightly floured hands, press out the dough into the
prepared flan pan or pie plate.
3 Make the filling: mix together the almonds, 50g /
2oz of the sugar, the orange zest and egg white.
Spread evenly over the shortcake. Drain the
apricots, reserving the juice, then arrange the
apricots on the filling. Bake for 25-30 minutes,
until lightly golden and firm to the touch.

4 Place the orange and apricot juices in a pan
with the remaining 2 tablespoons of sugar and
boil rapidly until reduced by half. Brush over the
warm shortcake and dust with a little icing sugar.
5 Serve warm, with the remaining syrup if you
like.

Variation:
Try putting a spoonful of grated orange or lemon
zest in the pastry mixture for extra flavour.
Replacing half the orange juice in the filling with a
similar quantity of Cointreau, or other orange-
flavoured liqueur, gives the cake quite a degree of
sophistication.

Lemon and lime pudding

This tangy pudding separates during cooking to give a light, spongy topping with a delicious sauce underneath.

Serves 6

100g/3½oz unsalted butter,
 softened, plus more for greasing
175g/6oz caster sugar
finely grated zest and juice of
 3 lemons
finely grated zest and juice of 1 lime
4 medium eggs, separated
50g/2oz plain flour
100ml/3½fl oz milk
icing sugar, for dusting

1 Preheat the oven to 180ºC / 350ºF / gas 4. Grease a 1.4 litre / 2½ pint deep ovenproof dish. Cream together the butter and sugar until light and fluffy. Stir in the lemon and lime zest and juice and the egg yolks (the mixture will curdle at this stage, but don't worry), then beat in the flour and milk.
2 In a separate bowl, whisk the egg whites until standing in soft peaks. Stir a quarter of the egg whites into the mixture to lighten it, then gently fold in the remainder.
3 Turn into the prepared dish. Stand the dish in a roasting pan with enough water to come 2.5cm / 1in up the sides of the dish. Bake for 30-35 minutes, until risen with a pale golden crust.
4 Dust with icing sugar and serve warm with pouring cream.

Pineapple puddings

These puddings are delicious served with a coconut-flavoured custard.

Makes 4

1 tbsp caster sugar
198g/7oz can of pineapple rings in
    their own juice
2 pieces of stem ginger in syrup
50g/2oz margarine or butter
50g/2oz light muscovado sugar
1 medium egg
75g/2¾oz self-raising flour
toasted flaked coconut, to serve

1 Preheat the oven to 180°C / 350°F / gas 4. Line the bases of four 175ml / 6fl oz ramekins with discs of greaseproof paper. In a heavy-based pan, dissolve the caster sugar in 2 tablespoons water. Boil until golden and pour into the ramekins.
2 Cut 2 of the pineapple rings in half and place a piece in each dish. Quarter one piece of the stem ginger and place a piece in the centre of each pineapple half. Chop the remaining pineapple and ginger.
3 Cream together the fat and sugar until pale and fluffy. Beat in the egg, fold in the flour, then stir in the chopped pineapple and ginger. Spoon into the ramekins and smooth the surface. Stand the dishes in a roasting pan with 2cm / ¾in of water and cook in the oven for 25-30 minutes until golden.
4 Run a knife around the edge of the puddings and turn them out on to individual plates. Discard the paper and sprinkle with toasted flaked coconut to serve.

Stuffed apple spirals

Serves 4

4 firm dessert apples, peeled and
    cored
butter for greasing
2 tbsp light muscovado sugar
40x7½ cm/16x3 inch strip of ready
    rolled puff pastry
beaten egg yolk, to glaze
hot, runny custard, to serve (page 40)
for the filling
2-3 tbsp seedless raisins
about 4 tbsp apple or other fruit
    brandy or Cointreau
good pinch of ground cinnamon
1 tbsp finely chopped mixed peel

1 Well ahead, put the raisins in a small bowl with just enough of the alcohol to cover and leave to plump up.
2 Preheat the oven to 200°C / 400°F / gas 6. Arrange the apples in a buttered ovenproof dish (paring off a small slice from the base, if necessary, so they will sit steadily) and sprinkle over half of the muscovado sugar. Bake for 7-10 minutes, or until the apples are partly cooked.
3 Make the filling: drain any excess alcohol from the raisins, if necessary, and mix them with the ground cinnamon and mixed peel. Pack the mixture into the cavities of the 4 apples and sprinkle with the remaining muscovado sugar.
4 Cut the pastry lengthwise into 4 long strips. Arrange each strip in a spiral around the outside of each apple as shown, with one end tucked underneath and the other twisted into a decorative flourish on top (which will also help hold the pastry in place). Using a pastry brush, paint the pastry lightly with the egg glaze.
5 Bake for 15 minutes or until the pastry is golden. Serve with hot, runny custard.

Fruity baked cheesecake

Serves 6

150g/5oz digestive biscuits, crushed
50g/2oz butter, softened
85g/3oz seedless raisins or sultanas
grated zest and juice of 1 lemon
450g/1lb mascarpone cheese
100g/3½oz sugar
2 egg yolks, beaten
2tbsp cornflour
200ml/7fl oz sour cream

1 Preheat the oven to 200°C / 400°F / gas 6. Grease a 20cm / 8in springform cake pan and line with baking paper. Place the crushed biscuits and butter in a bowl and mix until well combined. Transfer to the cake pan and press down well into the base to form a crust. Bake for 7 minutes, then leave to cool.
2 Put the raisins or sultanas and lemon juice in a small pan and simmer gently for 5 minutes. Drain well and set aside. In a large bowl, beat together the mascarpone and sugar until smooth. Stir the egg yolks into the mascarpone with the lemon zest, cornflour, sour cream and fruit.

3 Pour the mixture into the prepared cake pan and bake for 45-50 minutes until golden. Allow to cool completely, then remove from the cake pan.

Variations:
Add more flavour to the biscuit crumb base by adding ½ teaspoon ground cinnamon, ½ teaspoon grated orange or lemon zest or 2 tablespoons cocoa powder.
While the cheesecake is still warm, sprinkle over a little ground cinnamon and/or nutmeg, followed by a good dusting of icing sugar.

The rugged terrain of Fruity baked cheesecake invites the mining of a mouthwatering interior, opposite.

Apricot and pecan cheesecakes

Serves 4

for the bases
100g/3½oz digestive biscuits, crushed
40g/1½oz pecan nuts, ground
40g/1½oz unsalted butter, melted
for the filling
200g/7oz soft cheese
6tbsp crème fraîche
2tbsp caster sugar
a few drops of vanilla essence
grated zest and juice of ½ lemon
2-3 fresh apricots, stoned and quartered
3tbsp apricot jam

1 Preheat the oven to 190°C / 375°F / gas 5. Make the bases: place the crushed biscuits, pecan nuts and butter in a bowl and mix until well combined. Press the mixture firmly into the base and sides of four 9cm / 3½in loose-bottomed fluted flan pans. Bake for 7-10 minutes, just until the biscuit bases start to colour, then leave to cool.
2 Place the cheese, crème fraîche, sugar, vanilla essence, lemon zest and most of the lemon juice in a bowl and beat until smooth.
3 Remove the biscuit bases from their flan pans and fill them with the cheese mixture. Chill for at least 2 hours until firm.

4 Scatter the apricot quarters on top of the cheesecakes. Warm the jam in a pan with the remaining lemon juice, then brush the fruit with this glaze. Chill again before serving.

Variations:
Instead of fresh apricots, use ready-to-eat dried apricots, plumped up briefly in a little fruit liqueur or juice.
Try adding a thin layer of good-quality apricot jam between the crumb base and the filling.

Baked blueberry cheesecake

This is best made a day in advance to allow the flavours to develop.

Serves 8

for the biscuit base
85g/3oz digestive biscuits
25g/1oz pecan nuts
40g/1½oz butter, plus extra for
    greasing
25g/1oz plain chocolate, broken
    into pieces

for the filling
250g/9oz curd cheese
250g/9oz cream cheese
grated zest of 1 lemon and juice of
    ½ lemon
2 eggs
100g/3½oz caster sugar
seeds of 1 vanilla pod
350g/12oz blueberries
1 tbsp plain flour

1 Make the base: butter a loose-bottomed 23cm / 9in round cake pan. Place the digestive biscuits and the pecan nuts in a food processor and process until fine or chop the nuts and crush the biscuits with a rolling pin. Melt the butter and chocolate in a small bowl set over a pan of hot water (not boiling). Stir this into the biscuit mixture, then spread over the base of the cake pan and chill.

2 Preheat the oven to 180ºC / 350ºF / gas 4. Make the filling: sieve the curd and cream cheeses into a bowl and add the lemon zest and juice, the eggs, caster sugar and the vanilla seeds. Beat to a smooth batter.

3 Toss the blueberries in the flour, then fold them into the batter. Pour over the base and bake for 35 minutes, or until just set. Turn off the oven, leave the door ajar and allow the cheesecake to cool in the oven. Chill for a few hours or, preferably, overnight.

Raisin and vanilla cheesecake

Serves 6-8

for the base
175g/6oz plain flour
100g/3½oz butter, plus more for
    greasing
85g/3oz caster sugar

for the filling
50g/2oz unsalted butter
85g/3oz caster sugar
450g/1lb curd cheese
3 eggs
1tsp vanilla essence
25g/1oz cornflour
150g/5oz thick Greek-style yoghurt
85g/3oz seedless raisins
icing sugar and ground cinnamon, for
    sprinkling

1 Preheat the oven to 160°C / 325°F / gas 3.
Lightly grease a 20cm / 8in loose-bottomed cake
pan and line the base with baking paper. Make
the base: sift the flour into a bowl, cut the butter
into small pieces and rub it into the flour using
fingertips. When the mixture has the consistency
of fine breadcrumbs, stir in the sugar. Then
sprinkle the mixture evenly over the base of the
cake pan. Press down lightly with the back of a
spoon and bake for 20 minutes.

2 Meanwhile, make the filling: beat the butter and
sugar until light and fluffy. Add the curd cheese
and beat well. Beat in the eggs, one at a time,
then stir in the vanilla essence, cornflour, yoghurt
and raisins.

3 Set the cake pan on a baking sheet and pour in
the mixture. Bake for 50-60 minutes until firm
around the edges. Leave to cool in oven.

4 When the cheesecake is quite cool, chill it until
ready to serve, sprinkled with icing sugar and
cinnamon.

Orange chocolate chip cheesecake

100g/3½oz butter, plus extra for
    greasing
100g/3½oz caster sugar
450g/1lb soft cheese
2 eggs, separated
finely grated zest of 2 oranges
50g/2oz ground almonds
4tbsp plain flour, sifted
115g/4oz dark chocolate chips
icing sugar and cocoa powder, to
    decorate

1 Preheat the oven to 180°C / 350°F / gas 4 and
lightly grease a 20cm / 8in round springform cake
pan. Cream the butter with the sugar until pale
and fluffy.

2 Beat in the soft cheese, the egg yolks, orange
zest, almonds and flour until smooth. Whisk the
egg whites until standing in stiff peaks and then
fold them into the mixture. Lightly fold in the dark
chocolate chips.

3 Spoon the mixture into the prepared cake pan
and bake for 50-60 minutes, until golden brown,
firm to the touch and coming away from the sides
of the pan. (If the cheesecake starts to colour too

fast, cover it loosely with a double layer of
greaseproof paper.) Leave to cool in the cake pan
for about 1 hour.

4 Carefully remove the cheesecake from the cake
pan. Dust the whole top of the cheesecake lightly
with icing sugar and then dust the centre with
cocoa powder or use a template to make a
decorative pattern. Serve cut into slices.

Variations:

For an intriguing reversal, try colouring the
cheesecake mixture with 2 tablespoons of cocoa
powder and using white chocolate chips.

New Orleans bread and butter pudding with whiskey sauce

Serves 8

300ml/½ pint single cream
300ml/½ pint milk
1 vanilla pod
100g/3½oz caster sugar
4 eggs, beaten
1tbsp bourbon or Irish whiskey
1tsp ground cinnamon
16 thin slices of French bread
50g/2oz butter, plus more for
    greasing
85g/3oz raisins
25-50g/1-2oz pecan nuts, chopped

for the whiskey sauce

1tsp cornflour
150ml/¼ pint single cream
25g/1oz caster sugar
2tbsp bourbon or Irish whiskey

1 Preheat oven to 180ºC / 350ºF / gas 4 and butter a shallow ovenproof dish. Measure cream and milk into a pan. Split vanilla pod down its length, scrape out seeds and chop. Add pod and seeds to milk. Heat gently until just boiling, take off heat, cover and leave for 10 minutes.

2 Whisk together sugar and eggs until frothy, then whisk in warm milk mixture. Stir in whiskey and half the cinnamon. Spread both sides of each slice of bread with butter, then arrange slices in dish so they are slightly overlapping. Sprinkle with raisins and strain custard over bread, making sure it is evenly soaked. Let stand for 10 minutes.

3 Sprinkle pecans and remaining cinnamon over top of pudding and bake for 40-45 minutes until custard has set and top looks crisp and golden.

4 Make the sauce: blend cornflour to a paste with a little of the cream. Place in a small pan and mix in the remaining cream, sugar and whiskey. Heat gently, stirring, until slightly thickened. Simmer for 2-3 minutes before serving with the pudding.

Louisiana bread pudding

This fragrant spicy version of the old favourite has the texture of a very moist fruit cake. Look out for dried cranberries in the dried fruit section of your supermarket – they soak up the milk well and add a wonderful sweetness to this recipe.

Serves 6

450g/1lb wholemeal bread, crusts
   removed
600ml/1 pint milk
115g/4oz butter, melted, plus more
   for greasing
175g/6oz soft dark brown sugar
4tsp mixed spice
2 medium eggs, beaten
350g/12oz mixed dried fruit (e.g.,
   currants, cranberries, sultanas,
   raisins, candied peel)
grated zest and juice of 1 orange
½tsp freshly grated nutmeg
2tbsp demerara sugar
crème fraîche, maple syrup and
   cinnamon sticks, to serve (optional)

1 Preheat the oven to 180°C / 350°F / gas 4. Grease a 25x12.5x6cm / 10x5x2½in cake pan or 1.25 litre / 2 pint ovenproof dish and line the base with baking paper. Tear the bread into small pieces and put in a bowl with the milk. Leave to stand for 30 minutes, then beat until smooth.
2 Stir in the butter, sugar, mixed spice, eggs, dried fruit and orange zest and juice, and beat well. Pour into the prepared cake pan or dish. Sprinkle over some freshly grated nutmeg and demerara sugar and bake for 1¼ hours, until risen and a skewer inserted into the centre of the cake comes out clean. Turn out and remove the lining paper.
3 Serve warm or cold, with crème fraîche, maple syrup and cinnamon sticks, if you like.

Brown bread pudding

Serves 4

8 slices of brown bread
2tbsp butter or sunflower oil
   margarine
2tbsp marmalade
85g/3oz mixed dried fruit
2 eggs
300ml/½ pint half-fat milk
1tsp ground cinnamon
pinch of freshly grated nutmeg
1tbsp light muscovado sugar

1 Preheat the oven to 200°C / 400°F / gas 6. Spread the slices of bread with the butter or margarine, then sandwich them together with the marmalade. Cut off the crusts and slice into triangles, arrange in a greased flan dish and scatter over the dried fruit.
2 Beat together the eggs, milk, cinnamon and nutmeg, and strain through a sieve over the pudding. Sprinkle over the sugar and bake for 25-30 minutes until crisp and golden. Serve hot or warm.

Variation:
You can use any combination of dried fruit for this recipe, and all kinds of sweet breads would work equally well, try malt loaf, brioche, currant bread or bara brith.

Roast pear parcels with ginger and caramel sauce

Serves 4

for the crystallized ginger
200g/7oz caster sugar
200g/7oz fresh root ginger, peeled
    and thinly sliced

for the pears
100g/3½oz butter
100g/3½oz caster sugar, plus more
    for sprinkling
3 William pears, cored and cut into 8
    wedges
2tsp fresh lemon juice
eight 20cm/8in square sheets of filo
    pastry
icing sugar, for dusting
mint sprigs, to decorate
vanilla ice cream, to serve (optional)

for the sauce
150g/5oz fresh root ginger, peeled
    and finely grated
250ml/9fl oz double cream
50g/2oz caster sugar

1 Make the crystallized ginger: dissolve the sugar in 200ml / 7fl oz water, stirring. Bring to the boil, add the ginger slices and poach in the syrup for 30 minutes.

2 Preheat the oven to 110ºC / 230ºF / gas ¼. Spread the drained ginger slices on a non-stick baking sheet. Put in oven for about 2 hours, until light brown and crisp. Remove and allow to cool. Increase the oven setting to 190ºC / 375ºF / gas 5.

3 Cook the pears: heat 50g / 2oz of the butter in a frying pan, then add sugar. Just before it turns a caramel colour, add the pears. Cook for 8-10 minutes, coating them in the caramel. Stir in 100g / 3½oz of the crystallized ginger (reserve the rest for decoration) and the lemon juice. Remove from the heat and allow to cool.

4 Melt remaining butter in a small pan. Brush a sheet of filo with melted butter and sprinkle with a little caster sugar. Lay another sheet on top. Place about 6 pear slices and some juice in the centre. Brush the pastry edges with melted butter and draw up the corners to make a pouch. Place on a lightly oiled baking sheet and brush with butter. Make three more parcels in the same way, then bake for 10-12 minutes, until golden.

5 Meanwhile, make the sauce: wrap the ginger in a clean cloth and squeeze the juice into a small bowl. In a pan, gently heat the cream to just below boiling point. In a separate pan, gently heat the sugar and 3 tablespoons of water until the sugar has dissolved. Increase the heat and bubble until mixture turns light golden. Slowly stir

in the hot cream and the ginger juice. Bring to the boil, then remove from the heat and strain.

6 Place a parcel on each serving plate, dust

with icing sugar and decorate with a mint sprig. Drizzle the sauce around and scatter around some crystallized ginger. Serve as it is, or with vanilla ice cream.

Baked apples

Serves 4

2 large dessert apples, such as Golden
  Delicious, cut across in half and cored
2tbsp light muscovado sugar
25g/1oz butter, plus more for
  greasing
for the filling
3 small tart crisp dessert apples, like Granny
  Smith
good pinch of ground ginger
1 egg yolk
1tbsp double cream
1tbsp brandy

1 Preheat the oven to 200°C / 400°F / gas 6. Arrange the apple halves in a buttered oven-proof dish and sprinkle over half of the muscovado sugar. Bake for 7-10 minutes, or until the apples are partly cooked.
2 Make the filling: peel and core the Granny Smith apples, then grate them into a small bowl and mix with the ground ginger, egg yolk, double cream and brandy.
3 Divide the grated apple mixture between the 4 apple halves to cover their cut surfaces completely. Sprinkle with remaining sugar and dot with pieces of butter.
4 Bake for 15 minutes or until the surface is golden and bubbling.

Baked stuffed pears

Serves 6

175g/6oz ricotta or low-fat cream
  cheese
175g/6oz Wensleydale cheese,
  grated
seeds from 1 cardamom pod, crushed
3tbsp clear honey
40g/1½oz unsalted butter
6 ripe pears
2tbsp pear or apple juice
1tbsp Calvados or brandy
fromage frais, to decorate

1 Preheat the oven to 200°C / 400°F / gas 6. Cream the ricotta or low-fat cheese with the Wensleydale, cardamom seeds, honey and 25g / 1oz of the butter, until smooth.
2 Peel, halve and core the pears, then press the cheese filling into the hollowed centres. Place pears in a baking dish just big enough to fit them snugly together in a single layer and dot with the remaining butter. Pour in the pear or apple juice and Calvados or brandy.
3 Cover with foil and bake in the oven for 30-35 minutes, until the pears are tender.

4 Place the pears under a preheated hot grill for 3-4 minutes, until they turn golden.
5 Serve hot with a sauce of the pan juices and decorated with fromage frais.

Variation:
Try this with some dolcelatte or Roquefort in place of the Wensleydale.

Peach popovers

Serves 4

75g/3oz plain flour
1 egg
125ml/4fl oz semi-skimmed milk
a little butter
200g/7oz can of peach slices in natural
   juice, drained and cut in half lengthwise
1tbsp caster sugar
¼tsp grated lemon zest

1 Preheat the oven to 220°C / 425°F / gas 7. Sift the flour into a bowl, make a well in the centre and break in the egg. Add half of the milk and gradually work into the flour with a wooden spoon. Beat the mixture until smooth, then beat in the remaining milk. The batter should have the consistency of thin cream.
2 Place a little butter in each compartment of a four-hole Yorkshire pudding pan. Heat in the oven for 1 minute until the butter has melted, taking care not to let it burn.
3 Pour the batter into the pudding moulds and add the peaches, divided equally. Bake for 20-25 minutes, until risen and golden brown.
4 Meanwhile, mix together the caster sugar and lemon zest and sprinkle over each popover just before serving.

Almond and orange baked apples

Serves 4

4 eating apples
grated zest and juice of 1 orange
4tbsp mincemeat
white of 1 egg, lightly beaten
40g/1½oz ground almonds
25g/1oz caster sugar
custard, crème fraîche or yoghurt, to
   serve

1 Preheat the oven to 200°C / 400°F / gas 6. Peel and core the apples, then brush with orange juice. Fill the centre of each apple with mincemeat, making sure that you pack it down well.
2 Put the egg white into a small bowl. Mix the almonds, sugar and orange zest in a separate bowl. Coat the apples in the egg white, then in the almond mix, until they are completely covered.
3 Place the apples in a buttered ovenproof dish and bake for 50-60 minutes until the apples are tender and the coating is crisp and golden brown.
4 Serve hot with custard, crème fraîche or yoghurt.

Peach clafoutis

The clafoutis is a classic French fruit dessert. A cross between a plump pancake and a pudding, it is very easy to prepare and makes a perfect winter dessert served warm.

Serves 6

3 large eggs
150g/5oz plain flour
100g/3½oz icing sugar, plus a little
  for dusting
300ml/½ pint skimmed milk
1tsp vanilla essence
butter, for greasing
400g/14oz can of peaches in
  natural juice, drained
grated zest of 1 lemon

1 Preheat the oven to 190ºC / 375ºF / gas 5. In a bowl, beat together the eggs, flour, sugar, milk and vanilla essence.
2 Cover the base of a 20cm / 8in greased baking dish with the peaches and sprinkle over the lemon zest. Pour in the batter and bake for 35 minutes, or until the batter is firm.
3 Dust with some icing sugar and serve warm.

The clafoutis treatment works equally well with fresh peaches, or try the classic version with black cherries, unstoned for fuller flavour.

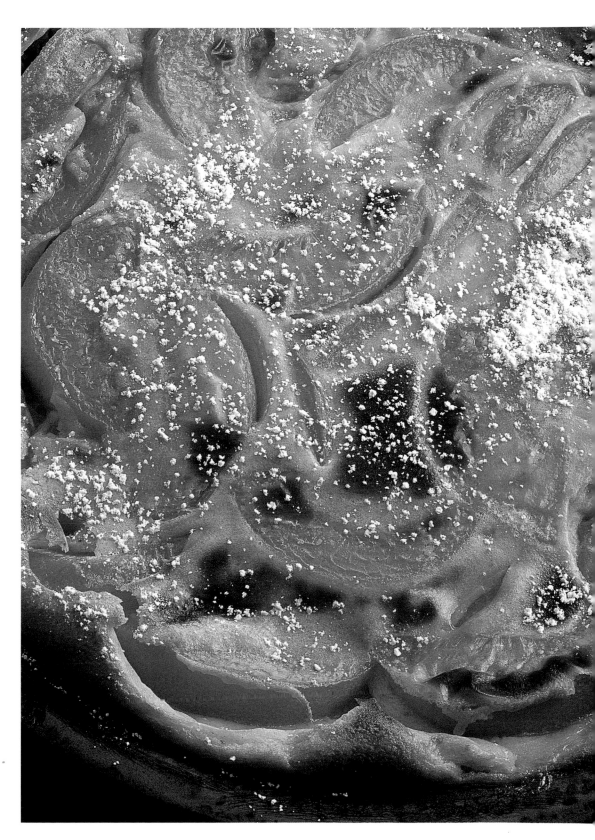

Master class: making steamed puddings

Orange marmalade steamed pudding

Serves 4

100g/3½oz unsalted butter, plus more for greasing
2tbsp golden syrup
grated zest and juice of ½ orange
100g/3½oz caster sugar
3 eggs, lightly beaten
3tbsp orange marmalade
85g/3oz self-raising flour
1tsp baking powder
1tsp cinnamon
85g/3oz fresh white breadcrumbs
pouring cream or custard, to serve

1 Lightly grease a 1.25litre / 2pint pudding basin. Mix the golden syrup with the orange zest and juice, and pour and spoon into the bottom of the pudding basin (2).
2 In a large mixing bowl, cream together the butter and sugar until light and fluffy. Beat in the eggs, a little at a time, until incorporated. Stir in the orange marmalade.
3 Sift together the flour, baking powder and cinnamon and fold into the creamed mixture with a large metal spoon. Fold in the breadcrumbs (3).
4 Spoon the mixture into the prepared pudding basin. Cover the top with 2 layers of greaseproof paper and a layer of foil (4), all three pleated across the middle (this will allow the pudding to expand during the cooking process).
5 Tie securely with string around the top of the basin and secure an extra length of string to form a handle. Place in a steamer, or sit on an upturned saucer in a large saucepan. Pour in enough boiling water to reach halfway up the sides of the pudding basin. Cover with a tight-fitting lid and steam for 2 hours – the water should simmer gently. Check regularly

to make sure the pan doesn't boil dry, and only top up with boiling water.
6 Carefully lift out the pudding basin (5 & 6) and remove the foil and greaseproof paper from the pudding (protecting your hands from

the steam). The pudding should be firm to the touch. Test with a skewer – it should come out clean. Leave the pudding to cool slightly before turning out.
7 Serve hot with pouring cream or custard.

Individual chocolate and hazelnut puddings

You can use either metal dariole moulds or deep ramekin dishes for this recipe. Tea cups may also be used to good effect.

Makes 6

100g/3½oz unsalted butter,
   softened, plus extra for greasing
85g/3oz chopped hazelnuts, toasted
4tbsp maple syrup
100g/3½oz plain chocolate, broken
   into small pieces
100g/3½oz light muscovado
   sugar
3 eggs, lightly beaten
85g/3oz self-raising flour
1tsp baking powder
1tbsp cocoa powder
85g/3oz fresh white breadcrumbs
more maple syrup and pouring cream
   or custard, to serve

1 Grease 6 individual dariole moulds or ramekins. Mix 3 tablespoons of the toasted hazelnuts with the maple syrup. Place a teaspoonful of the mixture into the bottom of each mould.
2 Place 85g / 3oz of the chocolate in a small heatproof bowl. Set the bowl over a pan of gently simmering water and heat gently until the chocolate has melted.
3 Cream together the butter and sugar until light and fluffy. Gradually beat in the eggs. Sift together the flour, baking powder and cocoa powder and fold into mixture with a large metal spoon. Stir in the melted chocolate, the remaining chocolate pieces, the hazelnuts and, finally, the breadcrumbs.

4 Spoon the mixture into the dariole moulds or ramekins, until each is two-thirds full. Cover the tops of the moulds with foil and stand in a steamer or place in a large saucepan. Pour in boiling water to reach halfway up the sides of the moulds.
5 Cover the pan and simmer for 30-40 minutes, until the sponges have risen to the top of the moulds. Remove the foil. The sponge should be firm to the touch.
6 Turn out and serve with extra maple syrup and pouring cream or custard.

Opposite: **The unholy trinity (clockwise from the top left): Pear and almond steamed pudding; Ginger, lemon and honey steamed sponge; and Individual chocolate and hazelnut puddings.**

Ginger, lemon and honey steamed sponge

Serves 6

100g/3½oz unsalted butter,
   softened, plus extra for greasing
2tbsp honey
5cm/2in piece of stem ginger, finely
   chopped, plus 1tbsp of its syrup
1 lemon, rind and pith removed, thinly
   sliced
100g/3½oz caster sugar
3 eggs, lightly beaten
85g/3oz self-raising flour
1tsp baking powder
85g/3oz fresh white breadcrumbs
1tbsp ground ginger
cream or custard, to serve

1 Grease the inside of a 1.25litre / 2pint pudding basin. Mix together the honey and ginger syrup. Pour into the bottom of the pudding basin. Press the lemon slices into the syrup on the bottom and use them to line the sides of the basin.
2 In a large mixing bowl, cream together the butter and sugar until light and fluffy. Beat in the eggs, a little at a time, until incorporated.
3 Sift together the flour and baking powder, and fold into the creamed mixture with a large metal spoon. Fold in breadcrumbs, stem ginger and ground ginger.
4 Cover and steam as described in the master class on the previous pages. Serve warm, with cream or custard.

Pear and almond steamed pudding

Serves 6

100g/3½oz unsalted butter, softened, plus more for greasing
2tbsp raspberry jam
2 pears, peeled, cored and chopped
1tbsp lemon juice
100g/3½oz caster sugar
3 eggs, lightly beaten
85g/3oz self-raising flour
1tbsp baking powder
85g/3oz fresh white breadcrumbs
50g/2oz flaked almonds, toasted
cream or custard, to serve

1 Lightly grease a 1.25litre / 2pint pudding basin and spoon the jam into the bottom. Toss the chopped pears in the lemon juice and leave to one side.
2 In a large mixing bowl, cream together the butter and sugar until light and fluffy. Beat in the eggs, a little at a time, until incorporated.
3 Sift together the flour and baking powder, and fold into the creamed mixture with a large metal spoon. Fold in breadcrumbs, pears and almonds.
4 Spoon the mixture into the prepared pudding basin. Cover and steam as per the master class on pages 130-1. Serve with cream or custard.

Variations:

You can use any type of good fruit jam in the bottom of the basin. A fine-cut marmalade will also work well.
Try tossing the pears in Amaretto or Cointreau, or other nut- or fruit-flavoured liqueur instead of the lemon juice.

Gingered fruit pudding

Serves 8

for the fruit filling
200g/7oz can of pineapple chunks in juice
2 bananas
2 ripe pears
50g/2oz light muscovado sugar
50g/2oz butter, cut into small cubes
for the pudding
100g/3½oz light muscovado sugar
100g/3½oz butter
2 eggs, beaten
175g/6oz wholemeal self-raising flour
½tsp bicarbonate of soda
2tsp ground ginger
100g/3½oz crystallized ginger or drained stem ginger, chopped
custard or crème fraîche, to serve

1 First make the fruit filling: drain the pineapple, reserving 3 tablespoons of the juice. Peel and slice the bananas. Peel, core and chop the pears. Mix the fruit, sugar and butter, then turn half of this mixture into a buttered, 1.75 litre / 3 pint pudding basin which has been lined with greaseproof paper.
2 Make the pudding mixture: beat the sugar and butter until light and fluffy. Beat in the eggs, a little at a time, then fold in the flour, bicarbonate of soda and ground and crystallized ginger. Stir in the reserved pineapple juice. Spoon half of the mixture into the pudding basin and smooth. Spoon the remaining fruit mixture over the top, then cover with the remaining pudding mixture and smooth the top.
3 Cover with greaseproof paper and foil (see pages 130-1), then steam for 2 hours until risen and firm. Allow to cool for 10 minutes, then turn out. Serve with custard or crème fraîche.

Apricot, pecan and pear pudding

Serves 8

for the topping
50g/2oz butter, plus more for
  greasing
50g/2oz light muscovado sugar
50g/2oz pecan halves, roughly
  chopped
100g/3½oz ready-to-eat dried
  apricots, roughly chopped

for the pudding
275g/10oz self-raising flour
100g/3½oz butter, cut into small
  cubes
100g/3½oz light muscovado sugar
1 pear, grated
2 eggs, beaten
100ml/3½fl oz milk
thick cream or ice cream, to serve

1 First make the topping: lightly mix the
ingredients, then spoon into a buttered 1.5litre /
2¾pint pudding basin.
2 Make the pudding: measure the flour into a
bowl. Add the butter and rub in with your
fingertips until the mixture has the consistency of
fine breadcrumbs. Stir in the sugar and pear, then
add the eggs and milk and mix to a soft batter.
Spoon over the topping and level the surface.
3 Cover with greaseproof paper and foil (see
pages 130-1), then steam for 1½-2 hours until
firm to the touch. Turn out and serve with thick
cream or ice cream.

Seven-cup pudding with a butterscotch sauce

A standard American measuring cup is the size of a large teacup – 250ml/8fl oz.

Serves 4

1 cup of seedless raisins or currants
1 cup of sultanas
1 cup of self-raising flour
1 cup of suet
1 cup of fresh breadcrumbs
1 cup of soft light brown sugar
1tsp ground cinnamon
1tsp mixed spice
1 cup of milk
1 egg, beaten
butter, for greasing
crème fraîche, to serve

for the butterscotch sauce

85g/3oz soft dark brown sugar
50g/2oz unsalted butter
150ml/¼ pint double cream
a few drops of vanilla essence

1 Mix the dry ingredients, then stir in the milk and egg until well combined. Pour into a buttered 1.25litre / 2pint pudding basin. Cover with a double layer of buttered foil, pleated across the centre, and secure with string.

2 Place the pudding basin in a large pan and half fill with boiling water. Bring the water to the boil, cover and steam for 2½-3 hours, checking the water level frequently. When almost ready, preheat the oven to 200°C / 400°F / gas 6.

3 Make the butterscotch sauce: heat all of the ingredients in a pan until the sugar dissolves. Bring to the boil and boil for 2-3 minutes until syrupy.

4 Turn the pudding out on an ovenproof dish. Pour over half the sauce and bake for 3-4 minutes until the sauce bubbles. Serve with crème fraîche and more of the sauce.

The caramelized apples filling the Apple flapjack pudding opposite, tumble invitingly from their hiding place.

Apple flapjack pudding

The lemon-scented apples are the perfect foil for the stickily sweet crust. Hot custard is the best accompaniment.

Serves 8

675g/1½lb eating apples
50g/2oz demerara sugar
grated zest and juice of 1 lemon
150g/5oz dark muscovado sugar
150g/5oz butter
4tbsp golden syrup
100g/3½oz self-raising wholemeal flour
225g/8oz porridge oats
2tsp ground cinnamon
2 eggs, beaten
custard, to serve

1 Quarter, peel and core the apples; cut each quarter into 3 slices. Place in a pan with the demerara sugar, lemon zest and juice. Heat gently, then cook for 5 minutes until the apples are just starting to soften. Remove from the pan with a slotted spoon, then boil the sauce until reduced and thickened. Pour the sauce over the apples.

2 Measure the muscovado sugar, butter and syrup into a small pan. Heat gently until the butter has melted, then allow to cool slightly. In a mixing bowl, mix together the flour, oats and cinnamon. Make a well in the centre and pour in the melted mixture and the eggs, stirring thoroughly to make a smooth batter.

3 Spread two-thirds of the mixture evenly over the base and sides of a buttered 1.5litre / 2¾pint pudding basin. Fill with the apples and spread the remaining mixture over the top. Cover with greaseproof paper and foil (see pages 130-1), then steam for 2 hours.

4 Allow to cool in the basin for 10 minutes, then turn out and serve with custard.

Chilling Out

A cool appraisal of frozen desserts

Master class: making ice cream

Vanilla ice cream

Serves 6
(makes about 700ml / 1¼ pints)

300ml/½ pint full-fat milk
1 vanilla pod
4 egg yolks
125g/4½ oz caster sugar
300ml/½ pint double cream

1 Pour the milk into a small pan. Using a
sharp knife, split the vanilla pod lengthwise
and scrape the seeds into the milk. Cut the
pod into several pieces and add to the pan.
Slowly bring almost to the boil, then remove
from the heat, cover and leave to infuse for
at least 15 minutes, but preferably
30 minutes if you have the time.
2 In a bowl, using an electric whisk, beat
together the egg yolks and caster sugar for
about 1 minute, until the mixture is thick and
creamy and leaves a distinct trail when the
whisk blades are lifted out. Bring the
flavoured milk back to the boil, then pour it
gradually into the egg mixture, stirring
continuously.
3 Pour the custard mixture into a clean,
preferably non-stick, pan and cook over a
very low heat, stirring continuously with a
wooden spoon until the mixture lightly coats
the back of the spoon. This will take 8–10
minutes. It is very important that you do not
allow the custard mixture to boil or it will
curdle.
4 Stand a clean bowl in another bowl filled
with ice, or with a mixture of ice and cold
water. Strain the custard mixture through a
sieve into the bowl, pressing down on the
vanilla pieces to extract all the flavour.
Leave the custard to cool for about 30
minutes, stirring occasionally to prevent a
skin forming. When completely cold, stir in
the cream. If time allows, chill the mixture
for 3 hours (or overnight if you prefer).
5 Start the ice cream machine running,
then pour in the mixture. (Go to step 6, if

you don't have a machine). Churn until it is
thick and has the consistency of softly
whipped cream. This will take about 30
minutes, depending on your machine, the
coldness of the mixture, and how long
your container has been in the freezer.
Spoon the mixture into a rigid plastic
container, cover and freeze until firm.
Transfer to the fridge 30 minutes before
serving.

6 If you do not have an ice cream machine,
freeze the bowl of cold or chilled custard for
about 2 hours until the mixture feels firm to
about 2.5cm from the edge. Remove from the
freezer and whisk well with a wire whisk to
break down the ice crystals. Return to the
freezer until semi-frozen, then whisk again.
Spoon into a rigid plastic container, cover
and freeze again until firm. Freeze for up to
2 months.

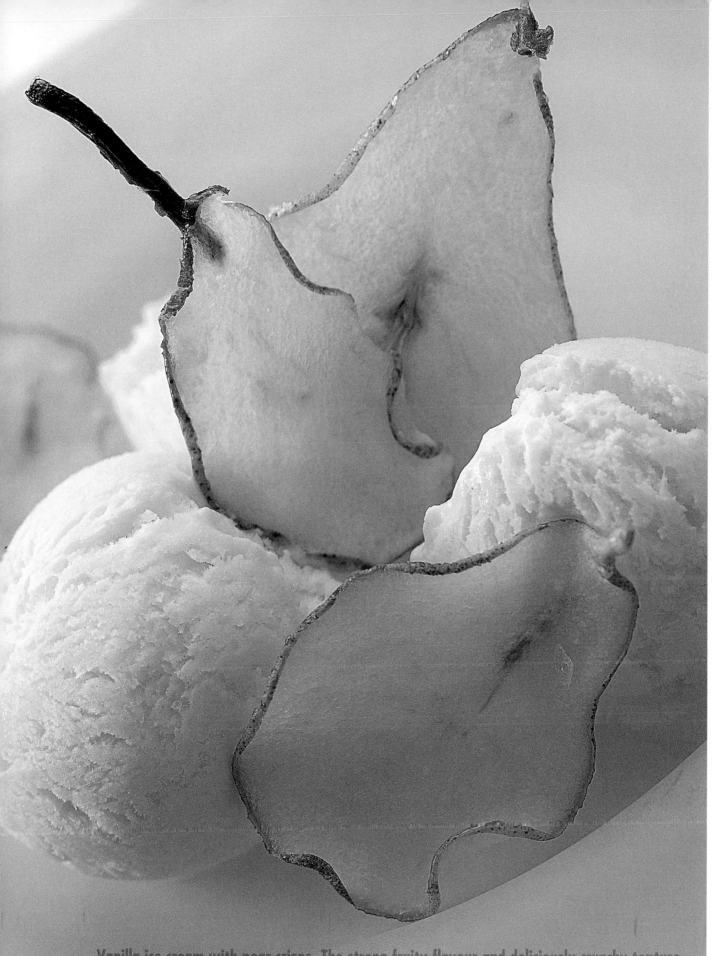

Vanilla ice cream with pear crisps. The strong fruity flavour and deliciously crunchy texture of Pear crisps (page 36) make them the perfect foil for good homemade vanilla ice cream.

Cappuccino ice cream

This is easy to make and great to have in your freezer for a luxuriously rich after-dinner pudding.

Serves 8

3 egg yolks
175g/6oz light muscovado sugar
300ml/½ pint semi-skimmed milk
1tbsp instant coffee granules dissolved
   in 2tbsp boiling water, cooled
125ml/4fl oz Amaretto liqueur
100g/3½oz amaretti biscuits, lightly
   crushed
100g/3½oz chocolate-coated
   coffee beans
1tsp cocoa powder, plus extra to dust
1tsp vanilla essence
450ml/¾ pint double cream
chocolate curls, to decorate (optional)

1 Put the egg yolks, sugar and milk in a glass or ceramic bowl and place over a pan of gently simmering water. Whisk for 5 minutes until pale and thick enough to coat the back of a wooden spoon, taking care not to let the custard boil. Allow to cool.
2 Stir the coffee, liqueur, biscuit pieces, chocolate beans, cocoa powder and vanilla essence into the cooled custard.
3 In a separate bowl, whip the cream until it forms soft peaks. Stir into the custard mixture.
4 Spoon into a rigid plastic container and freeze. Remove from the freezer after an hour and beat well. Leave for another hour, then beat again. Finally freeze until required.
5 Remove from the freezer 15 minutes before serving. Serve, dusted with more cocoa powder and decorated with chocolate curls, if you like.

Christmas ice cream

You can use any combination of dried fruits in this recipe.

Serves 6-8

25g/1oz sweetened dried
  cranberries
25g/1oz dried mango slices,
  chopped
25g/1oz ready-to-eat dried apricots
  chopped
25g/1oz seedless raisins, chopped
4tbsp brandy
600ml/1 pint double cream
65g/2½oz light muscovado sugar
75g/2¾oz fresh fine brown bread
  crumbs
25g/1oz pine nuts
½tsp ground cinnamon
fresh cranberries and bay leaves
  brushed with a little egg white and
  then dusting with caster sugar, to
  decorate (optional)

1 Put the cranberries, mango, apricots and raisins in a bowl, stir in the brandy and leave to soak.
2 Meanwhile, beat the cream and 15g/½oz of the sugar in a bowl until thickened. Transfer to a rigid plastic container and freeze, stirring every 30 minutes, for 2-3 hours, until almost set.
3 Preheat the oven to 200°C/400°F/gas 6. Mix together the remaining sugar with the breadcrumbs, pine nuts and cinnamon and spread over a baking sheet. Bake for 5-10 minutes until golden brown and caramelized. Leave to cool, then break up into small pieces.
4 Using a large metal spoon, fold the soaked fruit and breadcrumb mixture into the ice cream until well mixed, then freeze for 2 hours until set. If you wish, you can decorate it with 'frosted' cranberries and bay leaves.

Atholl brose ice cream

This ice cream is based on a luscious Scottish syllabub-type dessert made from oats, cream, honey and whisky.

Serves 12

600ml/1 pint milk
5 egg yolks
50g/2oz caster sugar
4tbsp clear runny honey, preferably
  heather honey
4tbsp whisky
50g/2oz medium oatmeal
50g/2oz granulated sugar
300ml/½ pint double cream

1 Bring the milk to just below the boil. In a heatproof bowl, whisk the egg yolks with the caster sugar until pale and thick, then stir in the hot milk.
2 Place the bowl over a pan of simmering water and stir until the mixture thickens enough to coat the back of a wooden spoon, about 30 minutes. Stir in the honey, leave to cool, then stir in the whisky.
3 Freeze the mixture in its bowl for 1 hour. Meanwhile, mix the oatmeal and granulated sugar on a baking sheet and toast under a preheated grill, removing frequently to stir with a fork, until the sugar caramelizes. Break into large crumbs

with a fork; leave to cool, then chill.
4 Whip the cream to soft peaks. Beat the partially frozen custard to loosen it slightly, stir in the oatmeal and fold in the cream. Return to the freezer for 1 hour.
5 Beat the ice cream again, transfer to an ice cream maker or suitable freezer-proof container and freeze until firm.

Strawberry ice cream

Serves 8

475ml/16fl oz milk
1 vanilla pod, split
6 egg yolks
75g/2¾oz caster sugar
400ml/14fl oz double cream
450g/1lb strawberries, hulled, plus
    extra to decorate
juice of 1 lemon
100g/3½oz icing sugar
mint sprigs, to decorate

1 Place the milk and vanilla pod in a pan and bring to the boil. Whisk the egg yolks and sugar together until thick and light. Stir in a little boiling milk to blend, then pour it into the pan. Cook over a low heat, stirring; do not allow to boil. When thickened, leave to cool and remove vanilla pod.
2 Transfer the custard to an ice cream maker and churn until thick. Add the cream and churn until frozen. Place the ice cream in a freezer-proof dish and freeze until required. Alternatively, place the custard in a deep baking dish, cover and put it in the freezer, stirring occasionally to prevent any large ice crystals forming. When

thickened, stir in the cream and return to the freezer.
3 Place half of the strawberries in a bowl with the lemon juice and icing sugar and mash with a fork. Roughly chop the remaining strawberries and stir into the mashed mixture. Transfer to an ice cream maker and churn until thick, or freeze in a baking dish as for the ice cream.
4 Fold the strawberry mixture into the ice cream, leaving it streaky – work quickly to prevent it from becoming too soft. Cover and transfer to the freezer for at least 2 hours, then decorate with more strawberries and mint sprigs.

Raspberry sorbet in strawberry tuiles with dried strawberry slices

If you have some cassis, add a couple of tablespoons to the raspberry purée – it really enhances the flavour.

Serves 8

500g/1lb 2oz raspberries
1tbsp clear honey
whites of 2 eggs
100g/3½oz caster sugar
for the oven-dried strawberry slices
250g/9oz ripe but firm strawberries, hulled
40g/1½oz caster sugar
for the strawberry tuiles (makes 20 biscuits)
100g/3½oz ground almonds
25g/1oz plain flour
70g/2½oz caster sugar
15g/½oz Oven-dried strawberry slices (as above), crushed
25g/1oz butter, melted and cooled, plus more for the baking sheets
white of 1 egg white, lightly whisked with a fork

(See the picture on page 138)

1 Purée the raspberries with 200ml/7fl oz water and honey in a food processor or blender. Pass the mixture through a sieve to remove the seeds.
2 If you have an ice cream maker, churn the raspberry mixture until it begins to freeze. Alternatively, put it in a rigid container and place it in the freezer (set to fast-freeze), until ice crystals form, then stir to break up the crystals.
3 Put the egg white and sugar into a clean, oil-free bowl and place this over a pan of hot water on a medium heat. With an electric hand-held whisk, beat the mixture until it forms a smooth meringue which can hold its shape, about 5 minutes.
4 Allow the meringue to cool, then carefully fold it into the freezing fruit mixture. Return to the freezer for about 3-4 hours, until completely frozen.
5 To make the oven-dried strawberry slices: preheat the oven to 110°C/230°F/gas ¼. Thinly slice the strawberries lengthwise. Arrange a layer in a bowl and sprinkle with a little sugar, repeat until all the slices are used up.
6 Carefully transfer the slices, one at a time, to a non-stick baking sheet. (It is important to use non-stick so that you can remove the strawberry slices when dried.)
7 Cook in the oven for 1½ hours, then turn the

slices over and cook for a further 1 hour until quite dry. Allow to cool. They can be stored in an airtight container or jar for up to 4 weeks.
8 To make the strawberry tuiles: in a bowl, mix the almonds, flour, sugar and dried strawberries. Add the butter and egg white to the mixture and stir in with a fork. Cover and chill for 30 minutes.
9 Preheat the oven to 160°C/325°F/gas 3. Butter 3 baking sheets, then place about 20 spoonfuls of mixture on them, spaced well apart.
10 Using a piece of plastic film to cover the piles of mixture, flatten into circles about 7.5cm/3in in diameter and 2mm/¹⁄₁₆in thick; remove the plastic film. Bake one sheet at a time for 8-10 minutes, until biscuits are golden at the edges.
11 Using a palette knife, remove the biscuits from the baking sheet while hot. Lightly press each one over a rolling pin to curl. Leave to harden for a few minutes, then transfer to a wire rack to cool. They can be stored in an airtight container for up to 2 weeks. If they become slightly soft, crisp them briefly in the oven.
12 About half an hour before you want to serve, transfer the sorbet to the fridge. Serve the sorbet nestling in the strawberry tuiles, decorated with the strawberry slices.

Peach and yoghurt ice cream

This custard-based ice cream can be made with other fruit, such as pineapple, gooseberries or nectarines.

Serves 4

3 egg yolks
150g/5oz caster sugar
150ml/¼ pint milk
8 large ripe peaches
3tbsp fresh lemon juice
150g/5oz thick Greek-style yoghurt
2tbsp amaretto or other almond liqueur (optional)

1 Beat together the egg yolks and sugar in a
bowl until pale. Heat the milk until almost
boiling, then pour it into the egg mixture,
beating continuously. Return the mixture to
the pan and cook gently, stirring, until
thickened – do not allow to boil. Allow to cool,
then chill.
2 Peel and stone the peaches, then purée half
of them with the lemon juice; finely chop the
rest. Stir the peach purée, yoghurt and
liqueur (if using it) into the custard. Pour the
mixture into a shallow plastic container and
freeze until it sets 2.5cm / 1in in from the
sides.
3 Turn the ice cream into a chilled bowl and
whisk to break down the ice crystals. Return
to the container and freeze for a further hour.
Whisk again, stirring in the chopped peaches,
then return to the freezer until firm.
4 Transfer the ice cream to the fridge about
30 minutes before serving to allow it soften
slightly. Serve with fresh fruit or a raspberry
or strawberry coulis made by puréeing the
fruit, straining it and sweetening it with a
little icing sugar.

Peach melba swirl

The Peach and yoghurt ice cream and Raspberry sorbet can be combined to spectacular effect for a special party dessert.

Serves 10-12

Peach and yoghurt ice cream (above)
Raspberry sorbet (left)

1 Make up one quantity each of Peach and
yoghurt ice cream and Raspberry sorbet until
both are just firm.
2 Fill a container with alternate scoops of ice

cream and sorbet, swirling together as you go,
then freeze until firm.
3 Serve in scoops to show off the swirls.

Griddled strawberries with lemon curd ice cream and lemon shortbread

Gary Rhodes' griddled strawberries with refreshing ice cream and melt-in-your-mouth shortbread is a temptation few can resist!

Serves 4-6

for the lemon curd (optional, makes about 650g/1lb 7oz)
225g/8oz caster sugar
225g/8oz unsalted butter
finely grated zest and juice of 3 lemons
5 egg yolks

for the ice cream
1 quantity lemon curd as above, or
   two 350g/12oz jars of ready-made
2 heaped tbsp crème fraîche
1 heaped tbsp natural yoghurt

for the lemon shortbread
100g/3½oz unsalted butter, plus more for
   greasing
50g/2oz caster sugar, plus more for
   sprinkling, if you like
finely grated zest of 1 lemon
140g/5oz plain flour

for the griddled strawberries
450g/1lb fresh strawberries
50g/2oz icing sugar
25g/1oz butter
fresh mint sprigs, to decorate (optional)

1 If you are making the lemon curd: place the sugar, butter, lemon juice and zest in a bowl over a pan of simmering water. Stir until melted, then beat vigorously until combined. Beat in the egg yolks and cook, stirring, for 15-20 minutes until thickened. Pour into a clean jar and cover with waxed paper or plastic film. Once cooled, seal tightly and store in the fridge. It will keep up to 2 weeks.

2 Make the ice cream: mix the lemon curd with the crème fraîche and yoghurt, and churn in an ice cream machine. Alternatively, freeze the mixture in a covered rigid container until set about 3cm / 1¼in from the edges. Whisk to break down the larger crystals, then

return to the freezer; repeat twice.

3 Make the lemon shortbread: preheat the oven to 180°C / 350°F / gas 4 and grease a baking sheet, then line it with baking paper. Cream the butter and sugar until pale and fluffy, then stir in the lemon zest. Sift the flour, then work it into the lemon butter. Using a piping bag, pipe the mixture on the baking sheet in 12 round or long shapes. Bake for 20 minutes until pale golden brown. Transfer the biscuits to a wire rack and leave to cool. Sprinkle with caster sugar, if you wish.

4 Make the sauce for the griddled strawberries: chop 4-5 strawberries and place in a pan with 2 teaspoons of icing sugar and 3 tablespoons of water. Stir over a low heat for 2-3 minutes, then press the mixture through a sieve into a bowl.

5 Heat a griddle pan over a high heat, then brush with the butter. Add the remaining strawberries and sift a tablespoon of icing sugar over the top. Cook for about 2 minutes, then turn the strawberries over and cook for 2-3 minutes.

6 Serve the griddled strawberries warm with the strawberry sauce, ice cream and shortbread. Decorate with mint, if you like.

Frozen strawberry yoghurt terrine

Serves 8

300ml/½ pint double cream
150g/5oz caster sugar
450g/1lb strawberries, hulled, plus
   extra to decorate
300g/10oz thick strawberry yoghurt

1 Chill a 1.25litre / 2pint loaf pan in the freezer. Whip half of the cream; spread three-quarters of it over the base and sides of the loaf pan. Return to the freezer and chill the remaining cream.

2 Dissolve the sugar in 175ml / 6fl oz water in a small pan. Bring to the boil and cook until the temperature reaches 107°C / 225°F on a sugar thermometer (or a drop of the syrup dropped in cold water forms a thread when pulled).

3 Roughly chop half the strawberries. Place them in a food processor or blender with the syrup and process until smooth, or mash to a purée, and stir in the syrup, followed by the yoghurt. Pour into an ice cream maker and

churn until thickened, or place in a deep loaf pan and transfer to the freezer, stirring occasionally, until thickened.

4 Chop the remaining strawberries; whip the remaining cream (but not the reserved chilled cream). Fold the strawberries and cream into the yoghurt mixture, then spoon into the cream-lined loaf pan. Freeze for several hours until firm. Spread the reserved chilled cream on top; return to the freezer until set.

5 Run the tip of a knife around the edge of the mould to loosen; dip the base in hot water, then invert on to a chilled plate. Smooth the cream with a palette knife, then decorate with more strawberries and serve at once.

Chocolate and chestnut parfait

Serves 6-8

150g/5oz amaretti biscuits, coarsely
   crushed
4tbsp brandy
225g/8oz sweetened chestnut purée
100g/3½oz dark chocolate, chopped
450ml/¾ pint double cream
for the coating
100g/3½oz dark chocolate
3tbsp double cream
for the decoration
50g/2oz dark chocolate
vegetable oil, for greasing
icing sugar, for dusting

1 Mix together the amaretti biscuits and brandy in a bowl and leave the mixture for 10-15 minutes until the brandy has soaked into the biscuits. Stir in the chestnut purée and the chopped chocolate.

2 Whip the double cream until it is stiff, then fold it into the chestnut mixture. Rinse a 900ml / 1½ pint pudding basin with cold water – don't dry it – and fill with the chestnut cream. Freeze for 12 hours or overnight, until firm.

3 Break up the chocolate for the coating and set in a small bowl with the cream over a pan of hot water, stirring gently until it forms a smooth sauce. Remove from the heat and let it cool.

4 Dip the parfait quickly into hot water, then turn out on a plate. Spread quickly with the chocolate coating, swirling it over the top and sides. Return to the freezer until it is firm.

5 Break up chocolate for the decoration and place in a bowl over hot water until melted. Spread over a board lined with lightly oiled foil and leave until just set. Cut out star shapes using a cutter or sharp knife; lift off using a palette knife.

6 Half an hour before serving, remove the parfait from the freezer and transfer it to the fridge to allow to soften. Just before serving, stick the chocolate stars into the top of the parfait and dust lightly with icing sugar.

Iced orange parfait with citrus sauce

If you don't have individual moulds, freeze the parfait in a loaf pan and serve cut into slices.

Serves 6

for the parfait
3 oranges
1/2 lemon
3 egg yolks
100g/3 1/2 oz caster sugar
1 tbsp Cointreau or other orange-
   flavoured liqueur
200ml/7fl oz double cream
100g/3 1/2 oz mascarpone cheese

for the citrus sauce
7 oranges
25g/1oz caster sugar
juice of 1/2 lemon
2 tsp cornflour
splash of Cointreau or other orange-
   flavoured liqueur

to decorate
70g/2 1/2 oz plain chocolate
cocoa powder, for dusting

1 Make the parfait: scrub one of the oranges and, without peeling it, cut it into chunks. Whiz in a food processor or blender until finely chopped. Press through a sieve. Squeeze in the juice from the remaining oranges and the lemon.
2 In a bowl, whisk the egg yolks and sugar until pale and thick. Stir in the fruit juices and transfer to a pan. Cook over a low heat, stirring until thick enough to coat the back of a spoon. (Don't let the custard boil or it will curdle.) Set aside to cool.
3 When the custard has cooled, add the orange liqueur. Transfer to an ice cream machine and churn until semi-frozen. Stir the cream into the mascarpone, then add to the machine and churn until frozen. Spoon the mixture into six 100ml / 3 1/2 fl oz moulds or ramekin dishes. Freeze for at least 2 hours.
4 Make the sauce: pare the rind from 2 oranges and cut into matchstick strips; squeeze the juice from these oranges into a small pan and add the rind. Add the sugar and

lemon juice. Simmer gently for 5 minutes, until the sugar has dissolved and the rind is tender. In a cup, blend the cornflour with 1 tablespoon of water, then mix in a little hot juice. Add to the pan and cook, stirring, for 1 minute until the sauce has thickened slightly. Add a splash of liqueur and allow to cool.

5 Peel the remaining oranges, removing the pith, then cut the oranges into segments (work over a bowl to catch the juice). Add the juice and segments to the sauce, cover with plastic film and chill.

6 Make the decorations: line a tray with greaseproof paper. Melt the chocolate in a heatproof bowl set over a pan of simmering water, or in the microwave cooker. Spoon into a small greaseproof paper piping bag, then pipe shapes on the prepared tray. Leave to set. When hard, peel away the paper.

7 Remove the parfaits from the freezer and dip each mould briefly in hot water. Run a knife around the rim, then turn out on to a freezer-proof tray. Return to the freezer.

8 About 30 minutes before serving, transfer the parfaits to the fridge to soften. Place one on each serving plate and surround with the sauce. Decorate with chocolate shapes and dust the plates with cocoa.

Variation:
To make parfait without an ice cream machine: tip the custard, liqueur, cream and mascarpone into a bowl and whisk until smooth. Pour into a shallow freezer-proof container and freeze for 1-2 hours, until the edges are just set. Scrape into a bowl and whisk again to remove lumps or ice crystals. Return to the container and freeze for 1 hour. Whisk again, then spoon into the ramekins and continue with the recipe. The parfait will not be quite as smooth as when made in an ice cream machine, but it will still be delightful.

Punch parfait with punch syrup and almond tuiles

Serves 10

6 tea bags
600ml/1pint boiling water
600ml/1pint red wine
600ml/1pint orange juice
juice of 4 lemons
650g/1lb 7oz caster sugar
6 eggs, plus 6 extra yolks
2tbsp dark rum
775ml/1pint 6fl oz whipping cream

for the almond tuiles

125g/4½oz unsalted butter, softened
150g/5oz icing sugar
whites of 3 eggs
125g/4½oz plain flour
50g/2oz flaked almonds

for the punch syrup

200ml/7fl oz red wine
1 cinnamon stick
a little grated nutmeg
juice of 1 orange
50-85g/2-3oz light muscovado sugar

1 Make the parfait: put the tea bags in a heatproof jug, pour over the boiling water and leave to infuse for 3 minutes. Strain into a pan and add the wine, citrus juices and 600g/1lb 5oz of the sugar. Bring to the boil, stirring to dissolve the sugar, then reduce gently to 600ml/1 pint. This will take about 1½ hours. Leave to cool.

2 In a bowl set over a pan of simmering water, whisk the eggs, extra egg yolks and remaining sugar until the mixture is light and leaves a ribbon on the surface when the blades are lifted out. Fold in two-thirds of the reduced liquid and the rum. Remove from the heat.

3 Whip the cream until it just holds its shape. Fold the remaining reduced liquid into the egg mixture, followed by the whipped cream. Pour into a rigid container and freeze for at least 4 hours, preferably overnight.

4 Make the tuiles: beat the butter and sugar together until light and fluffy. Stir in the egg whites, then fold in the flour and almonds. Chill until firm.

5 Preheat the oven to 180°C / 350°F / gas 4 and line a baking sheet with non-stick baking parchment. Spread some tuile mixture on the sheet in thin 10cm / 4in rounds, allowing

space around them for them to expand. Bake for 5-6 minutes until an even golden brown.

6 Allow to cool for a few minutes, then lift off the tray using a palette knife and drape over a rolling pin. When set, remove and allow to cool on a wire rack. Make the remaining tuiles in the same way.

7 Make the punch syrup: put all the ingredients in a pan and bring to the boil, stirring to dissolve the sugar. Reduce to a light syrup, then strain into a jug and cool.

8 Put tablespoons of the parfait in tuiles, arrange about 3 each on individual serving plates and pour a little syrup around to serve.

Semi-frozen strawberry bombes

Serves 6

2tbsp redcurrant jelly
225g/8oz strawberries
4tbsp freshly squeezed orange juice
25g/1oz caster sugar
50g/2oz amaretti biscuits, plus more
  to serve
450g/1lb mascarpone or cream
  cheese

1 Line 6 cups or ramekins with plastic film and gently warm the redcurrant jelly. Thinly slice 10 even-sized strawberries, dip each slice into the redcurrant jelly and press to the base and sides of the cups.
2 Chop or mash the remaining strawberries and mix with the orange juice and sugar. Place the biscuits between 2 sheets of greaseproof paper and lightly crush with a rolling pin. Fold the strawberry mixture and crushed biscuits into the mascarpone or cream cheese.
3 Fill the cups with the strawberry mixture, pressing it down lightly and smoothing the tops. Cover with plastic film and freeze for about 4 hours, or overnight, until firm. Transfer from the freezer to the fridge 1 hour before serving; the mixture should be softly frozen.
4 Turn the bombes out on to individual serving plates and peel off the plastic wrap. Serve with amaretti biscuits.

Snowball bombe

This is one of Josceline Dimbleby's favourite recipes for Christmas.

Serves 8

225g/8oz fromage frais
85g/3oz caster sugar
85g/3oz unsalted butter, melted
50g/2oz ready-to-eat apricots, diced
50g/2oz hazelnuts, toasted and
    chopped
25g/1oz candied peel, chopped
grated zest and juice of 2 oranges
grated zest and juice of 1 lemon
8 trifle sponges
about 450ml/¾ pint freshly
    squeezed mandarin or orange juice
15g/½oz powdered gelatine
150ml/¼ pint whipping cream
holly sprigs, to decorate (optional)

1 Place the fromage frais in a bowl and beat in the sugar, then beat in the butter, a little at a time, until smooth. Stir in the apricots, hazelnuts, candied peel and grated orange and lemon zest.
2 Cut each sponge into three thin slices; use 3 or 4 slices to line the bottom of a 1.25 litre / 2 pint pudding basin. Spoon a layer of the fromage frais mixture on top, then add another layer of sponge and repeat until you end up with a sponge layer on top.
3 Pour the orange and lemon juices into a measuring jug and bring to just over 450ml / ¾ pint with the mandarin or orange juice. Pour the juice into a pan and heat through; remove from the heat, sprinkle in the gelatine and stir until it has fully dissolved. Strain slowly over the pudding

basin, allowing it to pour down the sides and between the slices of sponge by pulling the sponge back with a spoon; chill until set.
4 When well chilled, dip the pudding basin briefly in hot water and turn out on a serving plate. Whisk the cream until thick and use to ice the bombe. Decorate with holly sprigs if you wish. Chill until ready to serve.

Variation:
Instead of the dried apricots, you can use seedless raisins or sultanas that have been plumped up in orange juice or orange-flavoured liqueur.

Passionate orange bombe surprise

As you slice into Josceline's second bomb, a surprise mass of grated chocolate tumbles out.

Serves 8

juice of 1 lemon
a little under 150ml/¼ pint freshly
    squeezed orange juice
whites of 2 large eggs
pinch of salt
175g/6oz caster sugar
1tsp powdered gelatine
4 passion fruit
300ml/½ pint whipping cream
200g/7oz plain chocolate
Cape gooseberries, to decorate

1 Strain the lemon juice into a measuring jug, then strain in enough orange juice to make up to 150ml / ¼ pint. Whisk the egg whites and salt with an electric mixer or a hand-held mixer until they hold peaks.
2 Pour the citrus juice into a pan, add the sugar and gelatine and heat gently until dissolved. Increase the heat and boil rapidly for exactly 3 minutes.
3 Pour the citrus juice in a thin stream on to the whisked egg whites, whisking all the time at high speed. Continue whisking for several minutes until cool and thickened.
4 Halve the passion fruit and scrape out the flesh, including the seeds, on to the egg white mixture; whisk this in until smooth. Whisk the cream until thick but not stiff and, using a

spatula, gently fold into the egg white mixture.
5 Transfer to a 1.25 litre / 2 pint metal bombe mould or basin; spread the mixture up the sides with a slight dip in the centre. Freeze for at least 5 hours.
6 When the ice cream is firm, coarsely grate the chocolate. Scoop out the centre of the ice cream and set aside. Spoon the chocolate into the cavity until completely filled. Stir the reserved ice cream to soften it, then spread it over the chocolate; freeze again for at least 1 hour.
7 Dip the mould briefly in very hot water, loosen the top edges with a round-bladed knife and turn out on to a plate. Return to the freezer until ready to serve. Decorate with Cape gooseberries and serve immediately.

Strawberry Alaska

Serves 8

1 recipe-quantity of Strawberry ice cream (see page 144) or 700ml/1¼ pints good-quality dairy strawberry ice cream (not soft-scoop)
2tsp icing sugar
a few strawberries, to decorate
for the sponge
butter, for greasing
2 eggs
50g/2oz caster sugar
50g/2oz plain flour
for the meringue
whites of 4 eggs
175g/6oz caster sugar

1 Line an 17.5cm / 7in diameter bowl or pudding basin with 2 sheets of plastic film so that the film overlaps the edges. Fill the bowl with ice cream and press to make a fairly solid dome shape; fold over the film to cover the top. Freeze for at least 1 hour.
2 Make the sponge: preheat the oven to 220ºC / 425ºF / gas 7 and butter a 20cm / 8in round sandwich pan, then line the base with baking paper. Using an electric whisk, whisk the eggs and caster sugar until the mixture has thickened and doubled in volume and leaves a trail on the surface when the whisk blades are lifted (this will take about 5 minutes).
3 Sift the flour and carefully fold it into the egg mixture. Spoon into the lined sandwich pan, lightly spread it to the edges and bake for 8 minutes, until pale golden and springy to the touch. Allow to cool in the pan for 5 minutes, then

turn out, remove the paper and leave to cool completely on a wire rack. (Keep the oven on for the meringue.)
4 Make the meringue: in a clean, grease-free bowl, whisk the egg whites until they form soft peaks. Add 1 tablespoon of the sugar and whisk again until stiff. Using a metal spoon, fold in the rest of the sugar, trying not to knock out any of the air.
5 Place the cooled sponge on a lightly greased baking sheet or ovenproof plate. Invert the ice cream dome on the centre of the sponge and discard the plastic film. Using a tablespoon, cover the ice cream and sponge with the meringue, swirling it in patterns. Dust with icing sugar.
6 Bake for 6 minutes, until the meringue is set and tinged golden brown.
7 Serve immediately, with a few strawberries for decoration.

Short-baked Alaska

This dessert is really quick and easy to make. The trick is to make sure that, first of all, the ice cream is really well frozen.

Serves 6

300g/10½oz strawberry ice cream
3tbsp caster sugar
pinch of cream of tartar
whites of 4 medium eggs, at room temperature
1tbsp drinking chocolate powder

1 Preheat the oven to 230ºC / 450ºF / gas 8. Pack the ice cream into six 150ml / ¼ pint ramekins. Place in the coldest part of the freezer for about 15-20 minutes until hardened.
2 Meanwhile, mix together the caster sugar and cream of tartar. In a separate bowl, whisk the egg whites until stiff. Still whisking, add the sugar mix to the egg, a little at a time, until the mixture forms stiff glossy peaks.
3 Remove the ramekins from the freezer and quickly spoon the meringue mixture on top of the ice cream. Place in the oven and cook for 4-5 minutes, until the meringue is browned.
4 Remove from the oven, dust with the drinking chocolate powder and serve immediately.

Mellow Fruitfulness

A luscious medley of fruit desserts

Figs and clementines poached in port

Serves 4

150ml/¼ pint port
100g/3½oz granulated sugar
pared rind of 1 lemon
1 cinnamon stick
8 small fresh figs
4 clementines, peeled
to serve
crème fraîche
ground cinnamon

1 Place the port, sugar, lemon rind and cinnamon stick in a pan with 150ml / ¼ pint water. Heat gently, stirring, until the sugar has completely dissolved. Bring to the boil and boil rapidly for 3 minutes.
2 Open out the figs into 4 segments using a knife or leave them whole, if you prefer. Add to the syrup with the clementines; cover and poach for 6-8 minutes until tender. Transfer the fruit to a serving dish using a slotted spoon.

3 Remove the lemon rind and cinnamon stick from the syrup and discard them. Bring the syrup to the boil and boil rapidly until reduced by half. Pour over the fruit and chill.
4 Serve chilled, with crème fraîche dusted with cinnamon.

Pears baked in honey

Serves 6

6 firm pears
6 cloves
8 cardamom seeds, cracked
2 cinnamon sticks
for the honey syrup
2tbsp caster sugar
4-6tbsp clear honey
300-450ml/½-¾ pint boiling water

1 Preheat the oven to 200°C / 400°F / gas 6. Peel the pears, leaving the stalks in place and remove the cores. Stick a clove in each pear and lay them on their sides in an ovenproof dish. Scatter the cardamom seeds and cinnamon sticks on top of the pears.
2 To make the honey syrup, dissolve the sugar and honey in the boiling water and pour over the pears. The pears should be half covered in liquid.

Bake for about 1 hour or until tender, basting them occasionally. Serve hot or let the pears cool in the honey syrup.

Toffee strawberries

Makes 20

vegetable oil, for greasing
250g/9oz caster sugar
5tbsp liquid glucose
500g/1lb 2oz strawberries
packet of short bamboo satay skewers or ice-lolly sticks (beware of the sharp points of satay sticks if given to children)

(See the picture on page 154)

1 Cover a baking sheet with foil and oil it lightly. Place a small bowl of cold water and a pastry brush next to the hob.
2 Pour 100ml / 3½fl oz water into a heavy-based pan and add the sugar. Stir, then place over a low heat until the sugar is completely dissolved, without further stirring.
3 Where the sugar has bubbled up inside the pan, wash down with the pastry brush dipped in cold water. (This will prevent crystals forming.) Add the glucose and lower the sugar thermometer into the liquid. Partially cover the pan with a lid and cook over a high heat until the temperature

reaches 152°C / 305°F, or until the mixture turns pale golden. Remove from the heat and allow to cool slightly for 2 minutes.
4 Stick a wooden skewer or ice-lolly stick into the green part (calyx) of the strawberry, then dip and turn the strawberries in the toffee, letting any excess run off. Place the coated strawberries on the foil-covered baking tray and allow to set for about 5 minutes.
5 Serve immediately as the toffee will start to dissolve after an hour or so.

Poached apricots with vanilla syrup

The simplicity of Phil Vickery's recipe makes this a wonderful last-minute treat.

Serves 4

350g/12oz sugar
1 lemon
2 vanilla pods, split in half
24-36 dried apricots, soaked overnight in cold water and drained
50g/2oz chilled unsalted butter, diced
mascarpone cheese, to serve

1 In a pan, gently heat 600ml / 1 pint water and the sugar, stirring occasionally until the sugar has dissolved.
2 Pare the rind from the lemon and cut it into thin strips. Squeeze the juice from the lemon and add to the pan with the rind. Bring to the boil and cook for 1 minute, then remove from the heat.
3 Add the vanilla pods to the pan and stir well, then add the apricots and bring to the boil. Reduce the heat and simmer for 5 minutes.
4 Strain through a sieve into a clean pan; set the apricots and pods aside. Bring the syrup to the boil and boil for 2 minutes until it has slightly thickened. Increase the heat and gradually whisk in the butter. (Don't let the syrup get too thick; add a few tablespoons of water, if necessary.)
5 Place 6 to 9 apricots on each plate and top with a piece of vanilla pod, if liked. Spoon over the vanilla syrup.
6 Serve immediately, with spoonfuls of mascarpone.

Poached pears with chocolate sauce

Serves 4

4 firm pears, peeled
50g/2oz golden caster sugar
juice and pared rind of ½ lemon
100g/3½oz plain chocolate, broken into pieces
3-4tbsp double cream

1 Slice the pears in half, leaving the stalks intact, and scoop out the cores. Pour 450ml / ¾ pint water into a shallow pan, add the sugar, lemon juice and rind and heat gently until the sugar dissolves.
2 Bring the liquid to the boil, then add the pear halves and cover with a dampened disc of non-stick baking paper. Simmer for 10 minutes, or until the pears are tender when pierced with a knife. Leave to cool in the poaching liquid.

3 Place the chocolate in a small pan with 6 tablespoons of the poaching liquid and melt over a very low heat, stirring continuously, until smooth. Remove from the heat.
4 Divide the chocolate sauce between 4 dessert plates. Spoon little dots of the cream on each plate and feather with the tip of a skewer. Remove the pears from the poaching liquid, pat dry with kitchen paper and arrange on top of the chocolate sauce. Serve at once.

Caramelized pear brioche with almond custard

Serves 4

4 medium-ripe pears
25g/1oz unsalted butter
25g/1oz caster sugar
1tbsp Poire William or brandy
4 thin slices of brioche
fresh mint sprigs, to decorate
  (optional)
for the almond custard
2 egg yolks
25g/1oz caster sugar
125ml/4fl oz milk
125ml/4fl oz single cream
2tbsp ground almonds
a few drops of natural almond
  flavouring (optional)

1 Quarter the pears, peel them and remove the cores, then cut each piece in half.
2 Place the butter and sugar in a frying pan; cook over a medium heat for a few minutes until caramelized. Carefully add 150ml / ¼ pint water and bring to the boil.
3 Add the pear slices and cook for about 10 minutes over a high heat, shaking the pan occasionally and allowing the pears to absorb the syrup. Add the Poire William or brandy and cook for 1-2 minutes, shaking the pan until the pears are coated in a syrupy glaze.
4 Make the custard: beat the egg yolks with the sugar until pale. Warm the milk, cream and almonds until just below the boil. Pour the cream mixture over the egg yolks and mix well, then return mixture to the pan and cook over a very gentle heat without boiling, stirring continuously, for about 15 minutes until it is thickened. Stir in the almond flavouring, if using it.
5 Toast the slices of brioche. Serve them topped with the pears and with custard poured around each portion; decorate with some sprigs of mint if you like.

Caramel rice and plum compote

Flaked rice cooks more quickly than pudding rice and gives a slightly smoother texture. In this version, a crisp caramel replaces the traditional nutmeg 'skin' of a baked pudding.

Serves 6

for the caramel rice
900ml/1½ pints milk
75g/2¾oz flaked rice
100g/3½oz caster sugar
150ml/¼ pint single cream

for the plum compote
75g/2¾oz light muscovado sugar
675g/1½lb plums, stoned and
    quartered
1 cinnamon stick, halved
2 bay leaves

1 Put the milk in the pan with the rice and three-quarters of the sugar. Bring to just below the boil, reduce the heat and simmer gently for 20-25 minutes until thick and smooth.
2 Meanwhile, make the compote: put the muscovado sugar in a pan with 450ml / ¾ pint water and heat gently until the sugar has dissolved. Bring to the boil and boil for 3 minutes. Add the plums, cinnamon and bay leaves. Cover and simmer very gently for about 10 minutes, until the plums have softened.
3 Stir the cream into the rice and turn into a 1.25litre / 2 pint shallow heatproof dish. Sprinkle with the remaining sugar and cook under a moderate grill until the sugar has lightly caramelized.
4 Serve warm or cold with the compote.

Summer soup of red fruits in citrus sauce

There's no reason why you should limit this delicious dessert to summer as you can now buy frozen fruit all year long. Just leave to defrost for several hours and drain off excess juice.

Serves 6

juice of 2 grapefruit
juice of 2 oranges
juice of 2 lemons
2 passion fruit, halved, pulp and
    seeds scooped out and reserved
1 kiwi fruit, peeled and finely
    diced
6 strawberries, finely diced
1kg/2lb mixed red fruits, such as
    strawberries, raspberries,
    tayberries and redcurrants

1 In a large bowl, mix together the citrus juices and stir in the passion fruit pulp and seeds, the diced kiwi fruit and diced strawberries.
2 Arrange the red fruit in the centres of 6 serving plates. Spoon the citrus sauce and diced fruit mixture around the red fruits and serve the 'soup' at once.

Rhubarb compote

Orange and either ginger or cinnamon are perhaps the nicest flavours to combine with rhubarb, and they work especially well as a compote.

Serves 4

100g/3½ oz sugar
1 cinnamon stick or a few slices of
    fresh root ginger
450g/1lb rhubarb, chopped
juice and finely grated zest of 1
    orange
whipped cream or crème fraîche, to
    serve

1 Gently heat 600ml / 1 pint of water with the sugar, and stir until the sugar is dissolved.
2 Add the cinnamon stick or root ginger, then simmer for a few minutes – check it has a good flavour, then remove the spices and add the chopped rhubarb. Bring to a simmer, cover and cook for 2-3 minutes until just tender, but not collapsing.
3 Lift out the rhubarb with a slotted spoon and boil the syrup until it is thickened. Stir in the orange juice and zest, then pour over the rhubarb and leave to cool. Chill before serving, topped with whipped cream or crème fraîche.

Variations:
Try using lime zest and juice in place of the orange.
For a delicious combination, toss in some fresh sliced strawberries just before serving.

Bottling is an ideal way of storing excess summer fruit. It is particularly suitable for fruits that do not freeze well, but only bottle those in peak condition.

Spiced pears

Makes about 900ml/1½ pints

450g/1lb caster sugar
300ml/½ pint white malt vinegar
2.5cm/1in piece of fresh root ginger, sliced
5 whole cloves
1 cinnamon stick
pared rind and juice of 1 lemon
1kg/2lb pears

1 Place the sugar and vinegar in a preserving pan. Add the ginger, cloves, cinnamon and lemon rind to the pan, and cook over a low heat until the sugar has completely dissolved.
2 Peel the pears, halve and core them (or leave them whole if they are small), and rub them with a little lemon juice to prevent discoloration. Place the pears in the syrup, cover and simmer gently over a low heat until tender.
3 Pack the pears and a few of the spices into sterilized jars. Boil and reduce the syrup by half and pour over the pears, so it just covers the pears, leaving a 1cm / ½in space between the fruit and the lid.

4 Leave to cool, then seal and label with the date and its name. Leave for 1 month before eating, to allow the flavours to develop more fully.

Note:
There is no need to sterilize this kind of bottled fruit because the sugar and vinegar solution acts as a preservative. The pears will keep for up to 6 months in a cool, dark, dry place.

Variations:
Use the same method to make spiced apricots, peaches and apples, or try whole crab apples with their skins on. Cooking times do vary though.

Bottled cherries

Bottled fruit should be stored in kilner jars or jars with rubber seals and airtight, screw-top lids. To sterilize the jars, use new rubber seals and sterilize them in boiling water for 10 minutes.

Makes about 1.5 litres/2½ pints

225g/8oz caster sugar
1.5kg/3lb cherries, stalks intact
5-6tbsp brandy

1 Place the sugar and 600ml / 1 pint water in a pan. Bring to the boil, reduce the heat and leave to simmer for 4 minutes. Allow to cool and set aside.
2 Trim the stalks to 2.5cm / 1in and tightly pack whole cherries into sterilized jars. Mix the brandy with the syrup, then pour over the fruit to cover it completely, leaving a 1cm / ½in space between the fruit and the lid. Seal.
3 Line the base of a large, deep pan or fish kettle with a double layer of kitchen paper and stand the jars inside, making sure they do not touch each other. If in doubt, place some more folded kitchen paper between them as they may crack if they touch each other during cooking.
4 Pour in enough cold water to come just below the neck of the bottles, replace the pan lid and bring slowly to the boil. Reduce the heat and simmer gently for 30 minutes.

5 Remove the jars and set them on a wooden board to cool. (Do not place them on a cool surface or they will crack.) Label with the date and its name. They will keep for up to 6 months in a cool dark, dry place.

Variations:
* Bottled raspberries, tayberries, blackberries or a combination: follow the same method as for Bottled cherries above.
* Peaches, nectarines or apricots: leave whole or halve them. Blanch and peel the fruit first, then bottle as above.
* Pears and apples: peel, core and halve or quarter, then continue as for the cherries.
* Experiment by adding different liqueurs or flavourings to the syrup, such as half a vanilla pod, a few crushed cardamom pods or a cinnamon stick.

Nectarines with pomegranate

This is a refreshing dessert to serve after a rich, spicy or fatty meal.

Serves 4

1 pomegranate
4 nectarines, stoned and cut into
  wedges
2 large bananas, thickly sliced
1 large pink grapefruit or 2 blood
  oranges, segmented
300ml/½ pint fresh orange or
  pineapple juice
langues de chat biscuits, to serve
  (optional)

1 Halve the pomegranate, scoop out the seeds and pulp and add to a serving bowl with the remaining ingredients. Toss to combine and chill until required.
2 Serve with langues de chat biscuits, if you wish.

Variations:
Add some chopped fresh pineapple or diced mango flesh.

Poached peaches with pistachios

The sparkling wine gives a delicate flavour to the peaches, but you can use apple juice if your prefer. For special occasions, add a splash of fruit brandy or liqueur.

Serves 6

8 peaches
1 bottle of Asti Spumante, or
  700ml/1¼ pints apple juice
1 vanilla pod
2 red fruit tea bags
225g/8oz raspberries
50g/2oz shelled pistachio nuts,
  chopped

1 Pack the peaches in a single layer in a pan. Pour over the wine or apple juice and tuck a vanilla pod and the tea bags underneath a peach to prevent them floating to the surface. Cover and bring to the boil, then immediately turn off the heat and leave to cool completely.
2 Remove the vanilla pod and tea bags and discard. Peel and halve the peaches, remove the stones, then slice the flesh.
3 Put the peach slices in a serving dish with the raspberries and spoon over some of the poaching liquid. Serve the fruit sprinkled with the chopped pistachios.

Spiced fruit salad

Serves 2

25g/1oz butter
½ tsp coriander seeds, crushed
6 cardamom pods, lightly crushed
1 tsp ginger
¼ tsp cumin seeds
½ papaya, cut into slices
½ small pineapple, cut into wedges
4 physalis fruit, papery husk turned back
1 lime, cut in half, plus juice of ½ lime
2 baby bananas, halved
25g/1oz shredded coconut, toasted,
    to serve (optional)
generous scoop of vanilla ice cream or a
    spoonful of Greek-style yoghurt, to serve

1 Melt the butter in a large frying pan.
Stir in the coriander, cardamom pods,
ginger and cumin, and gently fry for 2-3
minutes.
2 Toss the papaya, pineapple, physalis
and lime, cut-side down, into the spiced
butter and fry for 5-8 minutes, turning
frequently, until softened and golden. Add
the bananas and cook for a further 2
minutes. Squeeze in the lime juice and
cook for a further minute.
3 Serve sprinkled with the toasted
coconut, if using it, and a generous scoop
of vanilla ice cream or a spoonful of
Greek-style yoghurt.

Deep-fried strawberries with blackcurrant sauce

Phil Vickery's recipe makes the most of not-too-ripe strawberries

Serves 4

100g/3½oz blackcurrants, defrosted
 if frozen
50g/2oz caster sugar
1tbsp fresh lemon juice
8 sheets of filo pastry, each
 measuring 20cm/8in square
20 not-too-ripe strawberries
1-2tsp balsamic vinegar
finely grated zest of 1 lime
1 beaten egg, for glazing
vegetable oil, for deep-frying
icing sugar, for dusting
ground cinnamon, more strawberries
 and mint sprigs (optional), to
 decorate

1 Make the blackcurrant sauce: place the blackcurrants, sugar and lemon juice in a food processor or blender and whiz until smooth. (Add a little water if the sauce is too thick.) Strain through a sieve into a bowl and set aside.
2 Lay one sheet of filo pastry on the work surface, then place another on top at a different angle to make a star shape. Place five strawberries in the middle of each star, sprinkle over a little balsamic vinegar and a quarter of the lime zest. Dust with icing sugar to taste. Brush the edges of the pastry with egg. Carefully bring up the edges and crimp together at the top seal. Repeat to make three more parcels.

3 Heat the oil to hot (150°C/300°F) in a deep pan or wok. Fry the parcels, one at a time, for about 4 minutes each until golden brown. Remove with a slotted spoon and drain on kitchen paper.
4 Spoon some blackcurrant sauce into the centre of 4 serving plates and place a filo parcel in the middle. Dust with icing sugar and cinnamon, and decorate with strawberries and mint sprigs, if you like.

Lemon, chocolate and berry roulade

Serves 8

oil, for greasing
4 medium eggs
125g/4½oz caster sugar, plus extra
 for sprinkling
½tsp vanilla essence
50g/2oz desiccated coconut
grated zest and juice of 1 lemon
175g/6oz plain chocolate
300ml/½ pint double cream,
 whipped
225g/8oz mixed berries (e.g.,
 redcurrants, tayberries, raspberries,
 strawberries), stalks removed, hulled
 and halved, if necessary
fresh mint and extra berries, to
 decorate
icing sugar, for dusting

1 Preheat the oven to 200°C / 400°F / gas 6. Lightly oil a 23x32.5cm / 9x13in Swiss roll pan and line it with non-stick baking paper.
2 Whisk together the eggs, caster sugar and vanilla essence with an electric whisk for 5 minutes until thick and frothy and the whisk leaves a trail. Fold in the coconut and lemon zest and pour into the prepared pan.
3 Bake for 12-15 minutes until firm. Leave to cool.
4 Lay a sheet of non-stick baking paper the same size as the Swiss roll pan on a flat surface and sprinkle with the extra caster sugar. Turn the roulade on to the paper and peel off the lining paper. Trim the edges of the roulade, then sprinkle over the lemon juice.
5 Melt the chocolate in a heatproof bowl set over a pan of simmering water, then spread it over the roulade. Leave to cool slightly. Spread two-thirds of the cream over the roulade and top with the fresh berries. Lift

the paper along one of the short sides and use to help roll up the roulade.
6 Decorate with the reserved cream, extra fresh berries and sprigs of mint. Dust with icing sugar to serve.

Fruit tuile baskets with sabayon

Serves 8

for the tuile baskets
whites of 2 medium eggs
100g/3½oz caster sugar
15g/½oz plain flour
115g/4oz roasted chopped
    hazelnuts
4tsp hazelnut oil
1 large firm orange
450g/1lb mixed red fruit (e.g.,
    redcurrants, raspberries,
    strawberries), stalks removed, hulled
    and sliced, if necessary
icing sugar, to dust

for the sabayon
2 medium egg yolks
40g/1½oz caster sugar
4tbsp sweet white wine

1 To make the tuiles: preheat the oven to 200ºC / 400ºF / gas 6. Cut eight 20cm / 8in squares of baking paper and draw a 12.5cm / 5in circle in the centre of each. Divide between 2 baking sheets.

2 Beat the egg whites in a small bowl with a fork until frothy. Stir in the caster sugar, flour, hazelnuts and hazelnut oil. Put one-eighth of the mixture on each circle and spread evenly to the edges of the circles. Bake for 5-8 minutes.

3 Quickly lift off the baking paper and shape into baskets using an orange as a mould. If the biscuits set hard before you've managed to shape them, return them to the oven for a couple of minutes until softened and repeat the process. When completely cool, arrange the fruit in the baskets.

4 To make the sabayon, place the egg yolks, caster sugar, wine and 2 tablespoons water in a large heatproof bowl set over a pan of simmering water. Whisk with an electric whisk for 7-8 minutes, until the mixture is thick and frothy.

5 Dust the fruit baskets with icing sugar and serve with the sabayon sauce.

Exotic fruit brûlée

Serves 6-8

a selection of exotic fruit, e.g. passion
    fruit, mango, persimmon, papaya,
    star fruit
juice of 1 lime
75g/2¾oz caster sugar
300ml/½ pint double cream
300ml/½ pint thick Greek-style
    yoghurt
50g/2oz golden granulated sugar

1 Halve the passion fruit and scoop out the seeds. Peel the mango, persimmon and papaya, and chop the flesh into small pieces. Slice the star fruit. Mix all the fruit with the lime juice and 25g / 1oz of the caster sugar.

2 Turn the fruit into the base of a shallow ovenproof dish. Whip the cream until stiff, then fold in the yoghurt and the remaining caster sugar. Spread evenly over the fruit, making sure it is completely covered. Smooth the top and chill for 2 hours.

3 Preheat a hot grill. Sprinkle the granulated sugar evenly over the cream and place under the grill until browned, turning it as necessary.

4 Serve immediately or chill for up to 4 hours.

Variation:
This is equally nice using a selection of summer berry fruit. Replace the lime juice with lemon or orange juice and put some grated zest from the fruit in the cream for the topping.

Fleet of Fruit

Fruit tempura

Serves 4

Whisk together 100g/3½oz self-raising flour, one teaspoon ground cinnamon and 200ml/7fl oz sparkling mineral water to make a smooth batter. Dip 200g/7oz halved strawberries, two diagonally sliced bananas and wedges of two peaches into the batter; shake off excess. Shallow-fry in hot vegetable oil for 2–3 minutes on each side until golden. Drain on kitchen paper and serve hot, lightly dusted with icing sugar.

Griddled peaches on toast

Serves 2

Brush a griddle pan with butter and cook two sliced peaches or four sliced apricots for 2–3 minutes on each side. Toast four slices of fruit bread. Mix 25g/1oz butter, one tablespoon of caster sugar and half a teaspoon of ground cinnamon; spread over the toast. Top with warm fruit, and dollop of thick cream.

Peppered melon and raspberry salad

Serves 4

Mix the cubed flesh of one small melon, 250g/9oz raspberries or loganberries, the juice of one orange and two tablespoons chopped fresh mint; chill. Top with ground black pepper, decorate with mint sprigs.

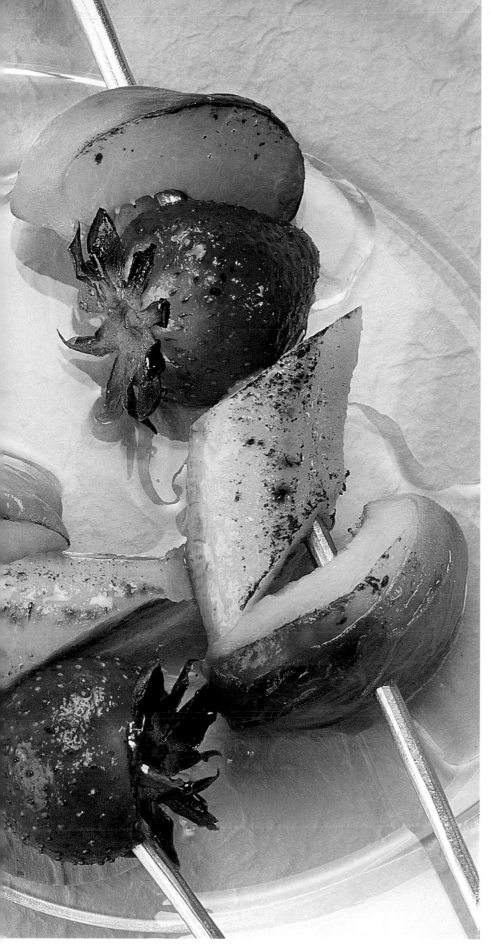

Fruit kebabs

Spear whole strawberries and slices of peach and banana on skewers. Brush with melted butter and barbecue or grill for 5 minutes, turning frequently until lightly browned. Drizzle with a little clear honey or maple syrup and serve warm.

Raspberry and ginger oat crunch

Serves 4

Divide 125g/4½oz raspberries between 4 wine glasses. Mix 500g carton half-fat Greek yogurt with two pieces of firmly chopped stem ginger and two tablespoons of the ginger syrup; spoon over the fruit. Chill, then top with two tablespoons of crunchy oat cereal over each to serve.

Acknowledgements

Most of the recipes in this book first appeared in *Good Food* or *Vegetarian Good Food* magazine. We are indebted to all those staff (past and present) involved in both magazines, and would especially like to thank Mary Cadogan for providing so many of the recipes.

Recipes by

Nadine Abensur
Plum, apricot and almond tart p88

Tom Aiken, Chef
Pear crisps p36, from the restaurant, Pied à Terre, Charlotte Street, London

Michael Barry
American breakfast pancakes p61, Pears baked in honey p157

Valerie Berry
Buttermilk pancakes with apple and pecan maple syrup p62

Angela Boggiano
Fruit pavlova p22, Hazelnut, banana and caramel nests p28, Saffron meringues with lemon syllabub p29, Exotic fruit layer p29, Pear and almond tatin p83, Orange marmalade steamed pudding p130, Individual chocolate and hazelnut puddings p133, Ginger, lemon and honey steamed sponge p133, Pear and almond steamed pudding p134

Angela Boggiano & Silvana Franco
Mascarpone and rum trifle p36, Cappuccino ice cream p142

Lorna Brash
Mississippi meringue pie p27, Waffles with date and orange compôte p62, Lemon, chocolate and berry roulade p166, Fruit tuile baskets with sabayon p168

Lorna Brash & Sue Townsend Clark
Peach and honeycomb fool p46, Almond palmiers with nectarine cream p46, Nectarines with pomegranate p164, Poached peaches with pistachios p164

Nicholas Bray, Junior Masterchef
Millefeuille of raspberries and Florentine biscuits p94 © Union Pictures Ltd

Orla Broderick
Meringue peaches p24, Summer fruit sabayon p48, Lemony crêpes p61, Mixed berry pie p75, Satsuma and raisin tart p75, French apple tart p76, Tropical mango tart p80, Paris-Brest p90,

Chocolate roulade p102, Brown bread pudding p125, Peach popovers p128, Poached pears with chocolate sauce p158

Sara Buenfeld
Coconut cream with Malibu fruits p47, White chocolate and blueberry jelly cheesecake p51, Dark chocolate puddings with white chocolate and Amaretto sauce p108

Mary Cadogan
Apple soufflé p11, Hot lemon soufflés p11, Chocolate praline soufflé with marinated summer fruits p12, Dark mocha soufflés with ice cream and mocha sauce p12, Nectarine mousse p18, White and dark chocolate mousse p20, Meringue Christmas tree p30, Redcurrant meringue roulade p30, Hazelnut meringue roulade with mango and orange cream p33, Raspberry syllabub trifle p38, Currants in red wine jelly p51, Crêpes Suzettes p58, Yorkshire curd tart p68, Pear crumble tart p71, Oranges and lemons basket p76, Smooth butterscotch tart p89, White chocolate choux puffs filled with lemon cream p92, Mincemeat, apple and marzipan strudel p96, Apple and pecan filo pie p97, Zuccotto p111, Lemon and almond cake p116, Raisin and vanilla cheesecake p123, New Orleans bread and butter pudding with whiskey sauce p124, Almond and orange baked apples p128, Gingered fruit pudding p134, Apricot, pecan and pear pudding p135, Apple flapjack pudding p137, Peach and yoghurt ice cream p145, Peach melba swirl p145, Chocolate and chestnut parfait p147, Semi-frozen strawberry bombes p150, Exotic fruit brûlée p168

R Chamberlain (reader)
Double-choc mud pie p113

Jacqueline Clarke
Basic pancakes p54, Orange pancakes with spiced fruit compôte p56

Ailsa Cruickshank
Pear and kumquat tart p73, Christmas ice cream p143, Figs and clementines poached in port p157

Gilly Cubitt
Caramelized banana tarts with vanilla custard p74, Pineapple puddings p119

Josceline Dimbleby
Apricot, rosemary and honey mousse p18, Snowball bombe p151, Passionate orange bombe surprise p151

Lewis Esson
Apple and cinnamon sugar crêpes p57, Tarte tatin p82, Stuffed apple spirals p119, Quick apricot and pine nut tatin p82, Orange chocolate chip cheesecake p123, Baked apples p127, Atholl Brose ice cream p143

Joanna Farrow
Strawberry mousse p20, Chocolate marquise slice p21, Passion fruit islands p24, Cherry and almond queen of puddings p27, Orange cheesecake brûlée with orange sauce p43, Instant fruit brûlée p43, Light lemon and nutmeg brûlée p44, Chocolate praline brûlées p45, Treacle tart p84, Amaretti and almond torte p87, Chocolate indulgence p93, Brandy snaps with chocolate cream p94, Chocolate brownie gâteau p100, Mocha roulade p104, Lemon and lime pudding p118, Caramel rice and plum compôte p160

Ursula Ferrigno
Almond and pear tart p66, Fig and lemon tart p66, Chocolate tart p104

Silvana Franco
Fruit tempura p170, Griddled peaches on toast p170, Peppered melon and raspberry salad p170, Fruit kebabs, Raspberry and ginger oat crunch p171

Linda Fraser
Rhubarb compôte p161

Jan Fullwood
Spiced fruit salad p165

Shirley Gill
Apricot and pecan cheesecakes p120

The Good Food Team
Spangled berry cream p48, Quick apricot fool p49, Profiteroles with chocolate sauce p92, Apricot almond shortcake p116

Peter Gorton, Head Chef
Dark chocolate mousse in a spiced tuile basket p17 from his restaurant, The Horn of Plenty, Devon

Kevin Graham
Louisiana bread pudding p125

Masayuki Hara
Roast pear parcels with ginger and caramel sauce p126

Ainsley Harriott
Banoffee pie p113, from his book, *In the Kitchen with Ainsley Harriott* (BBC Books)

Petra Jackson
Lacy peach crêpes p57, Filo apple strudels p97

Sybil Kapoor
Cranberry and almond tart p79

Sue Lawrence
Seven-cup pudding with a butterscotch sauce p137, from her book, *Entertaining at Home in Scotland*

Jane Lawrie
Cappuccino cups p112, Magic chocolate pud p112

Gill MacLennan
White chocolate cheesecake p107, Moist chocolate banana loaf p107, White freezer cake with sticky brownie base p109

John McQ
Short-baked Alaska p152

Maggie Mayhew
Blueberry and cranberry tartlets p78

Angela Nilsen
Soured cream apple crumb pie p79, Deep South sweet potato pie with toffee pecans p84, Glossy choc and peanut butter pie p87, Vanilla ice cream p140

Ian Parmenter
Peach clafoutis p129

Louise Pickford
Baked stuffed pears p127

Gary Rhodes
Chilled Valentine's mousse p17, Rhubarb and white chocolate trifle p38, Lemon crème brûlée with roasted peaches p40, Griddled strawberries with lemon curd ice cream and lemon shortbread p146

Michel Roux
Candied fruit soufflés p14, from his book, *Desserts* (Conran Octopus)

Bridget Sargeson
Raspberry sorbet in strawberry tuiles with dried strawberry slices p144, Strawberry Alaska p152, Toffee strawberries p157

Bill Sewell
Lemon and almond tart p72, from his book, *Food from the Place Below* (HarperCollins)

Jane Suthering
Chocolate brownies p100, Caramelized pear brioche with almond custard p159

Brigitte Tilleray
Tarte aux groseilles meringuée

Linda Tubby
Dovedale pear and pecan-puffs p80

Phil Vickery
Lace pancakes with raspberry and honey cream p56, Bitter chocolate tart with coffee bean syrup p71, Bitter chocolate puddings with chocolate fudge sauce p111, Punch parfait with punch syrup and almond tuiles p149, Poached apricots with vanilla syrup p158, Deep-fried strawberries with blackcurrant sacue p166

Mandy Wagstaff
Baked blueberry cheesecake p122, Strawberry ice cream p144, Frozen strawberry yoghurt terrine p147, Iced orange parfait with citrus sauce p148, Spiced pears p163, Bottled cherries p163

Tony Weston
Highland flummery p49, from his restaurant, the Taigh na Mara Vegetarian Guesthouse, Ullapool

Jenny White
Cranberry, pear and chocolate trifle with pear crisps p36, Fig and marsala trifle p37, Quick rhubarb tarts p81, Fruity baked cheesecake p120

David Wilson
Summer soup of red fruits in citrus sauce p160, from his restaurant, The Peat Inn, Fife

Mitzie Wilson
Tiramisu cheesecake p44

Photographers

Marie-Louise Avery
Iced orange parfait with citrus sauce p148

Steve Baxter
Magic chocolate pud p112, Apricot almond shortcake p117

Martin Brigdale
Michel Roux's Sauces (detail) p1, Exotic fruit layer p4 & p8, Lemony Crêpes p4 & p52, Fruit pavlova (detail) p9, Apple soufflé p10, Dark mocha soufflés with ice cream and mocha sauce p13, Making a soufflé step-by-steps p14, Candied fruit soufflé (detail) p14, Candied fruit soufflé p15, Chilled Valentine's mousse p16, Pavlova step-by-steps & detail p22, Fruit pavlova p23, Hazel, banana and caramel nests p28, Michel Roux's Sauces (detail) p35, Lemon crème brûlée with roasted peaches (detail) p40, Lemon crème brûlée with roasted peaches p41, Tiramisu cheesecake p44, Summer fruit sabayon p48, Quick apricot fool p48, Highland flummery p49, Bitter chocolate

tart with coffee bean syrup p70, Pear and almond tatin p83, White chocolate cheesecake p106, White freezer cake with stick brownie base p109, Stuffed apple spirals p119, Roast pear parcels with ginger and caramel sauce p126, Baked apples p127, Steamed puddings step-by-steps & detail p130, Orange marmalade steamed pudding p131, Individual chocolate and hazelnut puddings, Ginger, lemon and honey steamed sponge, Pear and almond steamed pudding p132, Ice cream step-by-steps p140, Vanilla ice cream with pear crisps (detail) p140, Vanilla ice cream with pear crisps p141, Poached apricots with vanilla syrup p158, Caramelized pear brioche with almond custard p159, Deep-fried strawberries with blackcurrant sauce p167, Fruit tempura p170, Griddled peaches on toast p170, Peppered melon and raspberry salad p170, Fruit kebabs p171, Raspberry and ginger oat crunch p171

Linda Burgess
Baked blueberry cheesecake p122

Peter Cassidy
Coconut cream with Malibu fruits p47, Punch parfait with punch syrup and almond tuiles p149

Polly Farquharson
Raspberry syllabub trifle p38

Ken Field
Spangled berry cream p48, Cranberry and almond tart p79, Plum, apricot and almond tart p88, Rhubarb compôte p161

Gus Filgate
Passion fruit islands p25, Meringue Christmas tree p31, White chocolate and blueberry jelly cheesecake p51, Lace pancakes with raspberries and honey cream p56, Lemon and almond tart p72, Pear and kumquat tart p73, Treacle tart p84, Dark chocolate puddings with white chocolate and Amaretto sauce p108, Lemon and lime pudding (detail) p115, Lemon and lime pudding p118, New Orleans bread and butter pudding with whiskey sauce p124, Almond and orange baked apples p128, Cappuccino ice cream p142, Christmas ice cream p143, Figs and clementines poached in port p156, Spiced pears p162, Bottled cherries p162, Exotic fruit brûlée p169

Christine Hanscomb
Cranberry, pear and chocolate trifle with pear crisps p4 & p34, Fig and marsala trifle p37

Alex Hansen
Dark chocolate mousse in a spiced tuile basket p16

David Jordan
Peach and honeycomb fool p46, Almond palmiers with nectarine cream p46, Caramelized banana tarts with vanilla custard p74, Nectarines with pomegranate p164, Poached peaches with pistachios p164, Spiced fruit salad p165

Graham Kirk
Mixed berry pie p75

Jess Koppel
Chocolate brownie gateau p5 & p98, Lemon and almond cake p5 & p114, Hot lemon soufflés p11, Chocolate marquise slice p21, Mississippi meringue pie p26, Currants in red wine jelly p50, Lacy peach crêpes p57, Chocolate indulgence p93, Brandy snaps with chocolate cream p95, Chocolate brownie gateau (detail) p99, Lemon, chocolate and berry roulade p166, Fruit tuile baskets with sabayon p168

William Lingwood
Toffee strawberries pp2-3, p5 & p154 (detail) p155, Raspberry sorbet in strawberry tuiles with dried strawberry slices p5 & p138 (detail) p139, Banoffee pie p113, Short-baked Alaska p152, Strawberry Alaska p153

Paul Moon
Crêpes à l'orange (detail) p58, Double-choc mud pie p113

James Murphy
Nectarine mousse p19, French apple tart p77, Deep South sweet potato pie with toffee pecans p85, Glossy choc and peanut butter pie p86, Mincemeat, apple and marzipan strudel p96, Roulade step-by-steps & detail p102, Chocolate roulade p103, Peach and yoghurt ice cream p145, Semi-frozen strawberry bombes p150

Alan Newnham
American breakfast pancakes p60

Ian O'Leary
Satsuma and raisin tart p75, Cappuccino cups p112

Thomas Odulate
Waffles with date and orange compôte p63

Nick Pope
Amaretti and almond torte p87

William Reavell
Quick rhubarb tarts p81

Roger Stowell
Bitter chocolate puddings with chocolate fudge sauce p7, Rhubarb and white chocolate trifle p39, Making cheesecake step-by-steps & detail p68, Yorkshire curd tart p69, Blueberry and cranberry tartlets p78, Tropical mango tart p81, Pear and walnut slices p81, Choux pastry step-by-steps & detail p90, Paris-Brest p91, Millefeuille of raspberries and Florentine biscuits p94, Bitter chocolate puddings with chocolate fudge sauce p110, Fruity baked cheesecake p121, Peach popovers p128, Gingered fruit pudding p134, Apricot, pecan and pear pudding p135, Apple flapjack pudding p136, Griddled strawberries with lemon curd ice cream and lemon shortbread p146

Kulbir Thandi
Peach clafoutis p129

Martin Thompson
Hazelnut meringue roulade with mango and orange cream p32, Making crème brûlée step-by-steps p40, Orange cheesecake brûlée with orange sauce p42, Chocolate praline brûlées p45, Pancakes step-by-step no3 & detail p54, Basic pancakes p55, Crêpes Suzettes step-by-steps p58, Crêpes Suzettes p59

Jerry Tubby
Summer soup of red fruits in citrus sauce p160

Struan Wallace
Meringue peaches p24

Philip Webb
Almond and pear tart p4 & p64 (detail) p65, Fig and lemon tart p67, Dovedale pear and pecan puffs p80, Chocolate brownies p101, Mocha roulade p105

Frank Wieder
Louisiana bread pudding p125

Simon Wheeler
Smooth butterscotch tart p89

Huw Williams
Pancakes step-by-steps (detail) p53, Pancakes step-by-steps p34

Whilst every effort has been made to trace and acknowledge all copyright holders, we would like to apologize should there be any errors or omissions.

Index